Fact-filled future?

EDITORIAL

46(01): 1/3 I DOI: 10.1177/0306422017703584

by **Rachael Jolley**

The "now" generation's thirst for instant news is squeezing out good journalism. We need an attitude change to secure its survival

THIS WORLD HAS never been in more need of good, well-researched journalism. It is tempting to write the words "old-fashioned" here too. And if by old-fashioned, what is meant is detailed, neutral, in-depth and well thought-out writing, then old-fashioned is what is called for.

Around the world there are squeezes from all directions, stifling what the public is allowed to know, and what it is allowed to say or write.

From government pressure to mafia threats, from commercial agencies to reputation-damaging (ro)bots, the right to speak and report is under huge pressure.

And good journalism must be there to unmask those threats.

With the rise of the words "fake news" comes a spirit that seems to think that I can apply this phrase to anything I disagree with. So the epithet "fake news" was out of its box and being used to try to disarm reporters and to undermine public belief both in research, experts, truth and often journalism.

So, this is a time for journalists and journalism to step up and do a really excellent, thorough job of discovering and publishing the news: that's not a news broadcast or publication that is just a hodgepodge of opinions based on very little research; nor a news story that has so much spin in it it's

hard to discern any actual facts.

There are those that might argue that the media has been through a pretty unimpressive period in the past 10 years, with some valiant exceptions. The line between the news and opinion pages has become increasingly hard to distinguish. So, it might be less than surprising that the public might have lost faith in news sources.

Social media has played a massive part in this. Hysterical opinion goes down a storm, instantly shared across platforms; while well-argued journalism, with more facts than screeching, tends to stay in its box, unread. And, of course, there are signs that attention spans are melting away. So not only does every item have to be now, now, now, but we can only be bothered to read the first line, or look at the picture.

Sadly, research from Stanford University shows young people are gathering their "news" from social media without bothering even to click through on a link. They also have trouble discerning the difference between a social media-placed advertising feature and a news story from a well-established news media company.

So shareable opinion has become king, and news has melted away and merged into a hybrid of what it once was. But journalists need to take back the news wherever →

→ they can, and re-establish it as a well-researched, investigated piece of information, not an outpouring of ill-informed thoughts.

And the public has to take some responsibility too. We need to be capable of a bit more dissection and scepticism when we see stories, rather than swallowing them whole without thinking. As our seasoned journal-

Hysterical opinion goes down a storm, instantly shared across platforms; while well-argued journalism, with more facts than screeching, tends to stay in its box, unread

ists explain in our Decoding the News special, everyone should be aware of techniques and tools to stop them being taken in, at least most of the time.

Meanwhile, journalists are doing some really strong investigations. As we go to press the BBC was broadcasting a story about truck drivers in the supply chain for furniture company Ikea, who were being paid less than the minimum wage, and being forced to live in their vehicles. They were drivers from Romania but working in Denmark, where they should have been paid according to Danish laws. The journalist was on the road talking to lorry drivers to find the story. Stories like these are hard to dispute, because the journalist has evidence to stand up the allegations.

Over in the Maldives, journalist Zaheena Rasheed, shortlisted for an Index journalism award this year (see page 37), is reporting about what is happening in the south Asian island country, despite a climate of fear.

And in other countries, remarkable reporters continue to make extraordinary efforts to get news out, despite dangerous conditions.

CREDIT: Ahmad Masood/Reuters

There are some signs that the world is starting to realise it needs good journalism. The New York Times saw a growth of 41,000 subscriptions in the week immediately after the election of President Trump. Sales of satire and news magazine Private Eye recently hit their highest level ever with 287,334 copies sold for one issue. Reports from Poland suggest a surge in sales of independent weekly Tygodnik Powszechny (see

our report on page 69). This in a country that is seeing its media freedom fall down global charts.

Jeremy Leslie, creative director of magazine-only shop Magculture in London, said he is seeing an upward tick in the sales of magazines "with serious intent". "More people are making [magazines with that type of content] and more people are buying it," he told Index on Censorship.

Is this a sign that some members of the public are learning at last that if they want journalism that tells them something they don't know (and isn't made up), they just might have to pay for it? Only time will tell. Otherwise, the survival of journalism looks fraught with danger. ⊗

Rachael Jolley is editor of Index on Censorship magazine. She tweets @londoninsider

ABOVE: In the aftermath of the 2015 earthquake a man reads a newspaper and his friend looks at his mobile phone in Kathmandu, Nepal

CONTENTS

INDEX ON CENSORSHIP

VOLUME 46 NUMBER 01 – SPRING 2017

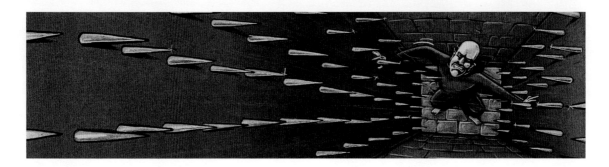

BRITISH
SOCIETY OF
MAGAZINE
EDITORS
AWARDS
2016
WINNER

EDITOR
Rachael Jolley
DEPUTY EDITORS
Jemimah Steinfeld, Sally Gimson
SUB EDITORS
Jan Fox, Tom Fearon, Sally Gimson,
Adam Aiken
CONTRIBUTING EDITORS:
Irene Caselli (Argentina), Jan Fox
(USA), Kaya Genç (Turkey), Natasha
Joseph (South Africa), Jemimah
Steinfeld

Index on Censorship | +44 (0) 20 7963 7262
292 Vauxhall Bridge Road, London SW1V 1AE, United Kingdom

EDITORIAL ASSISTANT
Kieran Etoria-King
DESIGN
Matthew Hasteley
COVER
Ben Jennings
THANKS TO:
Jodie Ginsberg, Sean Gallagher,
Ryan McChrystal

Magazine printed by Page Bros.,
Norwich, UK

Supported by
ARTS COUNCIL
ENGLAND

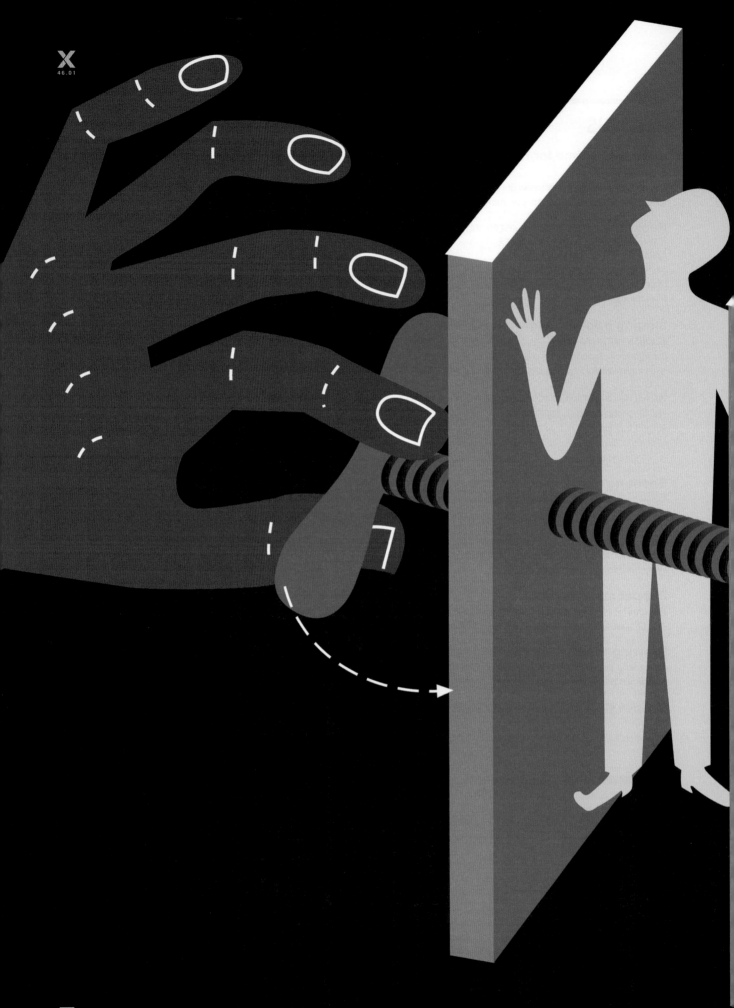

SPECIAL REPORT

CREDIT: Andrew Baker/Ikon Images

THE BIG SQUEEZE

Between a rock and a hard place

46(01): 8/10 I DOI: 10.1177/0306422017703585

Journalists in Mexico are facing threats from a corrupt government and violent cartels, and they can't always trust fellow reporters either, writes **Duncan Tucker**

"I HOPE THE GOVERNMENT doesn't give in to the authoritarian temptation to block internet coverage and start arresting activists," Mexican blogger and activist Alberto Escorcia told Index on Censorship magazine.

Escorcia had just received a series of threats for writing an article about recent unrest in the country. The next day the threats against him intensified. Feeling trapped and unprotected, he began making plans to flee the country.

Many people are concerned about the state of freedom of expression in Mexico. A stagnant economy, a currency in freefall, a bloody drug war with no end in sight, a deeply unpopular president at home and the belligerent Donald Trump administration freshly installed in the USA across the border, these forces are all creating a squeeze in 2017.

One of the biggest tensions is Mexico's own president. Enrique Peña Nieto's four years in office have brought sluggish economic growth. There has also been resurgent violence and a string of corruption scandals. In January this year his approval ratings plummeted to 12%.

But when journalists have tried to report on the president and his policies they have come under fire. For example, 2017 began with intense protests after Peña Nieto announced a 20% hike in petrol prices. Days of demonstrations, blockades, looting and confrontations with police left at least six people dead and more than 1,500 arrested. The Committee to Protect Journalists reported that police beat, threatened or briefly detained at least 19 reporters, who were covering the unrest in the northern states of Coahuila and Baja California.

News was not just suppressed, it was fabricated. Mass hysteria enveloped Mexico City as legions of Twitter bots incited violence and spread false reports of further looting, causing the temporary closure of 20,000 small businesses.

"I've never seen Mexico City like this," Escorcia said over the phone from his home in the capital. "There are more police than normal. There are helicopters flying above us every hour and you can hear sirens constantly. Even though there hasn't been any looting in this part of the city, people think it's happening everywhere."

Escorcia, who has investigated the use of bots in Mexico over the past seven years, believes the fake Twitter accounts were deployed to generate fear and to discredit and

I've had to suppress important information because they could have my family killed

distract from legitimate protests against the petrol hike and government corruption. He said he'd identified at least 485 accounts that repeatedly incited people to "ransack a Walmart".

"First they call on people to ransack shops, then they demand that the looters be punished and call for the army to be deployed," Escorcia explained. "This is a very delicate issue because it could lead to calls to censor the internet or arrest activists," he added, noting that the current administration has already had one thwarted attempt at establishing legislative powers to block internet access during "events critical to public or national security".

Days after the "ransack a Walmart" hashtag went viral, Benito Rodríguez, a hacker based in Spain, told Mexico's El Financiero newspaper that he had been paid to make it a trending topic. Rodríguez said he sometimes works for the Mexican government and admitted that it "might" have been a party that paid him to incite looting.

The Peña Nieto administration has long been suspected of using bots for political purposes. In an interview with Bloomberg last year, the Colombian hacker Andrés →

OPPOSITE: A demonstrator holds a placard during a recent protest against a fuel price hike in Mexico City. Police beat and threatened journalists who covered it, according to reports

Sepúlveda said that he'd been hired to influence the outcome of nine presidential elections across Latin America since 2005. These included Mexico's 2012 election, when he claimed Peña Nieto's team paid him to hack into the communications of their candidate's two closest rivals and lead an army of 30,000 Twitter bots to manipulate trending topics and attack the other contenders. The president's office issued a statement denying any relationship with Sepúlveda.

Mexico's journalists are also under threat from violent cartels. While researching his latest book Narcoperiodismo (Narco-journalism), the founder of Ríodoce newspaper, Javier Valdez, was struck by how common it now is for newsrooms at local papers to

Sepúlveda said that he'd been hired to influence the outcome of nine presidential elections across Latin America since 2005

be infiltrated by cartel spies and informants. "Serious journalism with ethics is very important in times of conflict, but unfortunately there are journalists who are involved with narcos," he told Index. "This has made our work much more complicated and now we have to protect ourselves from politicians, narcos and even other journalists."

Valdez knows full well the dangers of upsetting the powers that be. Ríodoce is based in Sinaloa, a sweltering state where the economy revolves around the drug trade. "In 2009 someone threw a grenade into the Ríodoce office, although it only caused material damages," he said. "I've had phone calls telling me to stop investigating certain murders or drug bosses. I've had to suppress important information because they could have my family killed if I mention it. Sources of mine have been killed or disappeared... The

government couldn't care less. They do nothing to protect you. There have been many cases and this keeps happening."

Despite the common problems they face, Valdez laments that there is little sense of solidarity among Mexican journalists or support from wider society. Moreover, as Mexico gears up for next year's presidential elections and continues to struggle with economic problems, he fears the pressures on journalists will only intensify, with grave consequences for the nation.

"The risks for society and democracy are extremely grave. Journalism can have a big impact on democracy and social consciousness, but when we're working under so many threats our work is never as complete as it should be," Valdez warned.

Without drastic change, Mexico and its journalists will face an even bleaker future, he added: "I don't see a society that stands by its journalists or protects them. At Ríodoce we don't have any support from business owners to finance projects. If we went bankrupt and shut down nobody would do anything [to help]. We have no allies. We need more publicity, subscriptions and moral support but we're on our own. We're not going to survive much longer in these circumstances."

Faced with a similarly tough situation, Escorcia shares this sense of urgency. Yet he remains defiant, tweeting after the latest threats against him: "This is our country, our home, our future and only by building networks can we save it. Telling the truth, uniting people, creating new media outlets, supporting existing ones, making public what they want to censor. This is how we can really help." ⊗

Listen to Duncan Tucker interviewed on the Index of Censorship podcast on Soundcloud, soundcloud.com/indexmagazine

Duncan Tucker is a freelance journalist, based in Guadalajara, Mexico

CREDIT: Elina Kansikas

Reality rapped

46(01): 11/12 | DOI: 10.1177/0306422017703586

Burkina Faso hip-hop star **Smockey** talks about writing lyrics that speak truth and aren't toned down to avoid upsetting someone

PLAYED AT THE opening of the Pan-African Film and Television Festival of Ouagadougou this year. It was my first time at the biggest African film festival and I was asked because the organisers didn't really have a choice any more.

Politicians and other important people were going to be there and they wanted to use me as an engaged artist, to give credibility to their events. They wanted my name. It gives a certain cachet, so they could say they're even working with artists who denounce them. But at the same time, they asked if I would water the wine, so to speak.

Before I played, they said: "Smockey, could you please avoid talking about politics? Can you avoid winding up the authorities?" But that never works. If you tell me that sort of thing, it only makes me want to say everything. They arranged it in such a way that I got to play for only five minutes because they didn't want to risk me playing for longer. I said: "Give me 10 seconds – that's all I need!"

→

ABOVE: Smockey at Index on Censorship's Freedom of Expression Awards 2016. His music was the soundtrack to a youth revolution, which saw a peaceful transition to democracy in 2015 in Burkina Faso

ABOVE: Smockey
performs at Index
on Censorship's
Freedom of Expres-
sion Awards 2016

→   It is a squeeze on freedom. The artist is a sponge and takes in everything. You
speak about what you know. I was born and
brought up in Burkina Faso and so I had lots
to say about the place, and I realised that
the problem was political. If the problem is
political then the solution is political. You
don't choose to be an artist or an activist
with a political pen – it happens because our
universe is extremely politicised, and all the
problems that you see are problems of bad
public management and of bad governance.

That's why nothing works. That's why
people are poor, why there is only primary
healthcare, why people have poor education
and why more than 60% of the population
is illiterate. That's why you have to raise
the consciousness of the masses so they
understand they don't have to put up with
a system that allows this and stops their
development. Music is the best way to raise
the consciousness of the people so they can
exercise their control as citizens.

They used to try to destroy artists by attempting to stop them expressing themselves,
but now they try to destroy artists by discrediting them, by not inviting them to appear on TV programmes or at public events.
They force activists to accept compromise,
another squeeze. The methods might change,
but it's still the same attempt at preventing
people from saying things and exercising the
control they should have as citizens.

It's a problem not just in Burkina Faso. It's
more difficult in countries where the repres-
sion is bloody. I'm thinking about Congo in
particular; Chad, where there is barely freedom or human rights; and even Cameroon.

Another pressure, or squeeze, is that people want you to sing things that give them
pleasure and make them dance, where they
don't have to think. There are people who
ask me why I write in gros français [the
French spoken by the elite in Africa]. "We
don't need that gros français," they tell me.
And I say: "What do you want me to do –
write differently?" I write what I feel. If there
is a part of the public that it resonates with,
that's enough.

But even if you have won things, and we
have certainly won things in Burkina Faso,
in terms of freedom in the public sphere, it is
still fragile and you have to convince people
that it is not over. It is more difficult today
to mobilise citizens because people think
they have won. We haven't won yet.

We are at the part which is called Évolution on my latest album, Pre'volution. The
first part is Prémonition, which is about
when the events are being prepared and we
are getting organised. The second part is Ré-
volution, which is the action itself. Évolution
is the most dangerous and delicate part. If it
is badly done, if it is badly executed, it is like
going back to the start.

But I'm an optimist. We have a constitution that says the president can be elected for
only two terms. The Regiment of Presidential
Security, a secret service organisation, has
been disbanded. The military junta no longer
runs the country. It is difficult now to impose
things by force and negotiation is needed. I
am optimistic about the future in Burkina. ⊗

*Smockey is the stage name of music producer
and political activist Serge Martin Bambara. He
was nominated as the Music in Exile fellow at
the Freedom of Expression Awards 2016*

*As told to **Sally Gimson***

Talking a tightrope

46(01): 13/15 | DOI: 10.1177/0306422017703587

In a divided Turkey, the Gezi legacy continues among those who are determined to be heard, writes **Kaya Genç**

WHILE STUDYING AT the School of Oriental and African Studies in London, Elif Bereketli was intrigued by fierce political debate about Turkey. After graduation, she returned to Istanbul to see the situation for herself. She found a complex society beyond the hardliners whose views often inform foreign perceptions.

"Turkey does not consist of seculars who can't stand the idea of living together with Muslims, and extreme Islamists who believe that anyone who has adopted the democratic programme of secularism should leave the country immediately," she said.

Bereketli now works as a journalist for Habertürk TV, where she is expected to be objective in her coverage of the cultural scene. It is a beat fraught with political divisions, with many seeing artists and authors as belonging to specific camps: secularist, conservative, republican and religious.

Turkey has historically been caught in the middle of cultural, political and religious forces. Wedged between the outer borders of the EU and the sectarian regimes of the Middle East, it has also come under historical influences of Islamism and European secularism.

Now, professionals like Bereketli are feeling the squeeze of different values, expectations and world views in society. Discussions about Turkish politics and culture skate on thin ice, requiring people to delicately balance politically opposing views.

Public discourse in Turkey started becoming more restrictive in the early 2000s when political correctness persuaded many it was better to be unheard than misheard. Ideas were suppressed and words carefully chosen as free speech entered a deep freeze.

While rhetorical finessing allowed some to share non-offending views, most people disengaged from public issues and retreated into silence.

Politics was left to opinion leaders at top newspapers as Brussels and Washington steered Turkey's political direction. Many extreme leftists and right-wing nationalists were jailed to quell dissent, either real or perceived. Those who strayed from safe topics in public speeches and writings were locked up; only the moderates existed. During this time, liberalism earned a bad name in Turkey as the vice that clamped down on ideas.

This fake liberal consensus that constricted the country in the name of keeping up with the "civilised world" ended spectacularly with the 2013 Gezi Park uprising. What started as an environmental protest escalated into what Turkish historian Şerif Mardin called "a climate of opinion" as progressives and conservatives clashed over the discourse of purported social agreement. Voices once silenced reached a deafening crescendo as substance returned to public speech.

"As someone who does not believe that values of one group are superior to those of others, I don't think the so-called →

ABOVE: A statue of founding president Mustafa Kemal Ataturk was removed from the main square in Rize in 2016 to be replaced by a monument to those killed in the 15 July coup attempt

→ polarised political atmosphere here changed my views, at least not on a conscious level," said Bereketli.

"When I express myself I take caution, remembering that I live with people who think differently and have values different to mine. I don't swear or put myself in a higher position [when] talking to my subjects. Nor do I claim that people who don't think like me are 'evil'. But I don't think this is about being Turkish or belonging to a certain culture. I think this is a universal notion."

Between 2008 and 2013, support for secularism and other founding principles of the Turkish republic ran afoul with critics who equated them with extremism. Similarly, Turkish nationalism was classified as a dangerous ideology; to some, even waving the national flag was deemed fascist.

The "squeeze" of political correctness made a mockery of freedom of expression. Supporters of leftist ideas and the principles of Turkey's founding father, Mustafa Kemal Ataturk, were stigmatised as "ultra-secularist extremists". Those who demanded an Asian direction were also criticised for views considered out of step with the modern Turkey.

The country was portrayed as consisting of "two big camps" where the only condition for harmony was for seculars and Islamists to keep their true feelings toward each other silent.

However, not everyone feels stranded in this no-man's-land.

"I don't see myself as someone balancing his views on political and cultural issues in Turkey," said Sernur Yassıkaya, an editor at the conservative daily Yeni Şafak.

"I express my thoughts freely through my opinion pieces in the paper and on social media. I don't see that much of a strict political divide in Turkey. Compared to the 1980s and 1990s, the cultural sphere here is much more free and vibrant."

Nevertheless, Turkey has become the world's biggest jailer of journalists, with nearly one third of the global total, according to a December 2016 report by the Committee to Protect Journalists.

Between August 2014 and March 2016, 1,845 people were prosecuted for insulting President Recep Tayyip Erdogan. In addition to anti-state charges, private citizens are flooding courts with defamation suits. In separate cases, Turkish pianist Fazil Say and the national NGO Atheism Association were both prosecuted for "insulting religious values", while last year a report by the Turkish Journalists Union found seven journalists had been convicted for defamation and five others subjected to other court action.

For a long time, the golden rule of "think before you speak" has been in place in Turkey. People must consider the implications of their words from different geopolitical and world-historical contexts. People must always balance what they say with appropriate counterweights. Catch yourself sounding too appreciative of the Western world, for example, and you might end up adding similarly appreciative statements about the East.

Saying something as ordinary as "Istanbul stinks the way Eastern cities do" can cast you as an outsider and cultural elitist. In a video posted to Twitter on New Year's Eve last year, Turkish fashion designer Barbaros Şansal infamously raised a glass to his country "which is now in deep shit" and voiced his happiness at being away from it. Şansal, who was in Cyprus when he made the video, was confronted by a mob upon returning to Istanbul and eventually convicted for inciting hatred on social media.

In the 1932 novel Yaban (The Strange), a classic of early republican fiction, Turkish author Yakup Kadri Karaosmanoğlu tells a similar if antiquated story of conflict. A Westernised intellectual from the capital Ankara visits eastern Anatolia where his modernising ideals clash with villagers' harsh religious fundamentalism.

Conservative literature, too, has portrayed the situation through pious characters from rural parts of the country, who struggle to fit in and express themselves when they move to secular metropolises. Characters in both genres try to fit in to the expectations of those with different views, failing to satisfy their expectations.

Despite the post-putsch crackdown, the legacy of Gezi continues among Turks determined for their voices to be heard. Their ideas challenge the traditional view of Turkey as a nation that can only survive through consensus.

Ideas were suppressed and words carefully chosen as free speech entered a deep freeze

"It is absurd to analyse Turkey as if 50% of people here belong to this one big group and the rest belong to another big group," Bereketli said.

"There are too many other frequencies and dynamics in the country. Exceptions to that purported ideological divide make up the majority of the country, not the minority." ⊗

Kaya Genç is a novelist and journalist based in Turkey. He is also a contributing editor at Index on Censorship magazine

Taking the bait

46(01): 16/17 | DOI: 10.1177/0306422017703588

Social media likes, fun photos and a drive for instant reaction are all part of the pressures on accurate reporting, writes **Richard Sambrook**

SERIOUS JOURNALISM IS suffocating. It is having the air squeezed out of it by rampant commercialism on one side and, on the other, the insistent demand for speed, strong opinion and impact in a 24/7 world. The old business models are failing and, as yet, there is no clear sign of an alternative for serious news that can measure the public interest against what simply interests the public.

The internet has undermined authority and trust in journalism, siphoning off audiences and advertising and diverting attention with sensation, trivia and – of course – "fake news". Trusted information is the currency of healthy democracies, but today that currency is debased, and we are all paying the price.

Look at the United States. Since the lifting of the "fairness doctrine" under Ronald Reagan in 1987 – which obliged broadcasters to be fair and balanced in their news coverage – partisanship in talk radio and the TV news networks has contributed to a polarised political environment and the election of a populist president. Ratings drive advertising and sensation drives ratings. The drama of Donald Trump's election campaign pushed viewing figures ever higher and ad revenues followed. As CBS chief executive Leslie Moonves stated: "[Trump's candidacy] may not be good for America, but it's damn good for CBS."

The wall between journalism's commercial and editorial operations is dissolving. Native advertising – PR disguised as journalism – is expected to be the new commercial saviour, from Buzzfeed to the New York Times. If the readers don't notice or care, does it matter if what we used to call advertising looks like news? Not always, but as PR, advertising, political activism and entertainment all blend together with journalism, it opens the door to exploitation and the "fake-news" panic we have had for the last few months. Too many members of the public can no longer tell the difference between those categories of information, largely because media companies are complicit in confusing them. A study at Stanford University found 82% of students couldn't tell the difference between sponsored content and independent news. In the UK, a YouGov survey for Channel 4 found only 4% of respondents could reliably tell real news from fake.

Social media and the technology giants bear a major part of the responsibility. Jonah Peretti, co-founder of Buzzfeed and the Huffington Post, recently said that social behaviour had changed media forever. For him, sharing is the key metric indicating user value, and his company is based on measuring and encouraging content that is shared.

That has clearly been very successful for many social media platforms. The problem is that sharing is a good indication of consumer value but not of citizen value. Sharing rewards sensation over authority, and encourages the clickbait online economy where it doesn't matter if something is true or not, just as long as you click on it and advertisers can ride on the back of your curiosity.

So a colourful lie will amass a million hits before the prosaic truth gets noticed. It used to be said in journalism, "if you are first and wrong, you are not first". Today, if you are one of the Macedonian teenagers manufacturing fake news to reap the ad revenue, you don't care.

The new economics of information and the weighting of sensation and immediacy over authority or accuracy has polluted public debate and left many citizens deeply confused about how the world works.

So what is to be done? The problem is that the two internet giants – Facebook and Google – that now dominate how we find out about the world are global, and largely unaccountable beyond their shareholders. And their boards are, of course, focused on the huge profits they generate rather than any wider social responsibility. However, there are signs that both are responding to perceived brand damage, rooting out fake news, tweaking algorithms, supporting media literacy programmes and helping search for a new economic model for journalism. These actions may ease part of the big squeeze on serious news, but there is a long way to go.

Some propose more foundation-funded public media. But such initiatives are usually small-scale, and not sustainable in the long term or replicable in countries that don't enjoy a large scale of philanthropy.

There are new initiatives from big media including more fact-checking services and, from the BBC, a commitment to "slow journalism", a deliberate turning away from the instant demands of Twitter to a longer and more considered approach to news. A welcome move, but one only a large public-funded organisation could afford to take.

There is a recognition that digital media has moved far ahead of most people's ability to understand it, so a renewed commitment to media literacy – understanding and

dissecting the media more widely – is important. Helping people think critically and recognise the qualitative difference between a tweet and a well-researched article from an accountable news organisation is crucial, but it is a long-term process.

In the meantime, we get the journalism we deserve. So think twice before you click "like" on a sensational headline from

When it comes to understanding the world, speed is a dubious virtue

a source you don't know – every time you do, you help fashion the media environment. Take out a subscription to a serious news organisation of your choice, because good journalism has to be paid for. And slow down – when it comes to understanding the world, speed is a dubious virtue. ⊗

Richard Sambrook is professor of journalism at Cardiff School of Journalism at Cardiff University, and former director of the BBC World Service

ABOVE: Members of the audience hold up their phones as Donald Trump speaks during an election campaign event in Tucson, Arizona

CREDIT: Thulani Mbele/Sowetan/Gallo Images/Getty Images

Dangerous minds

46(01): 18/21 | DOI: 10.1177/0306422017703589

As the Fees Must Fall movement in South Africa approaches its second anniversary, fears for the future of freedom of speech on campus are escalating. **Natasha Joseph** reports

were forbidden. Students were not allowed to enter the main administration building where supporters of the movement known as Fees Must Fall had previously held meetings.

Over at the University of KwaZulu-Natal's Westville (Durban) campus, a student described how police and private security guards had interrupted a gathering designed to discuss issues on campus in October 2016.

"The cops came in numbers and when they came, they pepper-sprayed us. They gave no warnings to students. They shot the students with rubber bullets and they brutally assaulted anyone who was coming from the library.

"I don't believe they are allowed to do that but they are forcefully entering. It's like they are instructed to stop students from expressing their views. They assault anyone standing in the way. They are instilling fear into the students."

But this was not a one-way battle to squeeze debate. In the weeks leading up to shutdowns at Wits, non-protesting students had been labelled "sell-outs" by those actively fighting for free education and decolonisation, and they found themselves under attack. Across the country, university buildings and vehicles burned. What had previously been a cohesive, united movement became fractious and its natural "enemy", university administrators, were not the only target. Students turned on each other, even within the movement.

Those vital spaces for debate, dissent and learning narrowed. The squeeze was on. One academic, who didn't want to be named, told Index that her faculty's staff room at a Cape Town university no longer buzzed with conversations between colleagues. "Everyone is too afraid to say anything that might be construed as political, so we just keep quiet instead," she said. "There's a really terrible climate of suspicion."

Student activist Thenjiwe Mswane began to realise that she could no longer align herself with Fees Must Fall because →

LEFT: A student offers flowers to police in a gesture of nonviolence during the #FeesMustFall protests in October 2016

AT THEIR BEST, university campuses are sites of debate, dissent and learning. But South African institutions are becoming increasingly uncomfortable and worryingly closed spaces where freedom of expression is threatened and the squeeze on open discussion is coming from more than one direction.

Towards the end of last year, it was common to see more police officers and armoured vehicles than students or academics at Johannesburg's University of the Witwatersrand (Wits). In an eerie echo of apartheid tactics, "gatherings" of any sort

→ the main organisers were unwilling to listen to a myriad of views. Last April Mswane took a stand against the exclusion of feminist and queer concerns. Armed with a heavy leather whip known as a *sjambok*, she confronted a group of male protesters at Wits. Photographs of what followed, which show Mswane being forcibly removed by a group of men, are evidence of what Christi van der Westhuizen, an associate professor at the University of Pretoria, has called an "anti-democratic element" in the student movement.

These campaigners seem to believe that you are either entirely for decolonisation or utterly against it. Mswane's commitment to the broader cause didn't matter to the men who physically attacked her when she questioned the absence of queer voices and black women's voices from the movement's work.

"I think that April was the last time that I would align myself with the movement that became #FeesMustFall. Not because it was not necessary, not because it was not valid, but because it was no different...from the movements of [black male protesters'] forefathers which were built on the blood drawn from the spines of black women. There is nothing new that happened on that day in April," she told Index.

In the months that have followed, the movement's celebrated cohesion has all but vanished. Mswane and others like her have withdrawn, leaving what was a robust, nuanced space for contestation filled with different voices down to just two sides. And those sides represent extremes: generally older, usually white academics vehemently opposed to the idea that European and other Western thinkers ought to be replaced by theorists from Africa and the rest of the global South versus those who want university curricula gutted of anything non-African.

Those somewhere on the middle ground are missing in action, often because they've been physically or verbally shouted out of the debate. Van der Westhuizen has written

about students at the University of the Western Cape who interrupted a debate involving Judith Butler and Wendy Brown, both known for radical critiques on present and historical forms of oppression. Students insisted they'd had enough of "white foreigners" telling black people what to do. Two local, black African academics – Achille Mbembe and Xolela Mangcu – were called "sell-outs".

Penelope Andrews is the dean of the University of Cape Town's law faculty. She noticed a definite shift during September and October when protests aimed at her institution and others peaked.

"It became increasingly apparent that nuance, reasoned dialogue, tolerance and moderation were casualties of the protests," Andrews told Index. "There were increasing demands – outright, subtle and clandestine – to either support the students, on the one hand, or condemn and penalise them, on the other.

"The middle majority – [non-protesting] students and staff – felt marginalised and silenced. The puzzling thing is that most, especially the students, I would argue, are deeply committed to the project of equity, transformation and social justice. They support the cause of accessible and affordable quality education, including free education, for the majority of students."

Despite this, UCT and several other universities had to delay their year-end exams and cancel some classes to stave off disruptions. Andrews was surprised by protesting students' attitude to the "sell-outs" who just wanted to get on with their work.

She was a student in South Africa during the apartheid era and was a protester herself during that time. But, she said, "the actual physical shutting down of the university is new to me. When I was a student at the (then) University of Natal in Durban in the late 1970s and early 1980s, ongoing protest against the apartheid regime was the currency at the university. We protested all the time. But we did not shut down the university as a tactic. Even with the slogan 'Liberation first, education later', the University of Natal continued to operate."

She added: "The shutting down of intellectual space is a different story. These actions emanate from across the ideological spectrum.

"From the conservative right, one observes a refusal to admit and confront the historical and contemporary vestiges of privilege and racism (the idea of "white innocence"), or the use of certain labels to silence (for example, accusing a speaker of using the race or gender card).

"From the political left, I would argue that there has been some silencing of individuals based on the practice of a kind of identity politics and the tension around who gets to represent and express the view of the relevant oppressed or subordinated group or individual."

Mehita Iqani takes a different view. She's associate professor of media studies at Wits and the founder of a podcast called the Academic Citizen. The "squeeze", she argued, isn't a genuine closing down of space so much as a number of "different iterations of free speech and healthy – though not always comfortable – debate".

"I have witnessed only a couple of 'closing down' moments," Iqani told Index. One of those was when the leader of the Wits branch of political party the Economic Freedom Fighters interrupted a peace meeting in a church and led a group of students in shouting at the vice-chancellor until he left.

She said: "I've seen a couple of mean Twitter comments from students directed at academic staff who dare to voice critique of student's tactics. I've seen academics on Facebook defriend colleagues that they claim are not progressive enough. But all of these are quite petty instances, I think. On a surface reading, it could be read as closing down debate, but I think more discussion and reflection tends to be generated as a result. Some

may become more polarised – the individual who defriended everyone he decided wasn't radical enough, for example – but in the bigger picture it gives us something to think with."

Thinking will be crucial in the coming months and years. The senate is any university's highest academic decision-making body and comprises full professors, senior management and a handful of elected representatives. Iqani, who serves as an elected member of the Wits senate, believes it's visible proof that change is crucial and that the real "squeezing" of debate has been perpetuated by those in power, not the student body.

She added: "Senate does not 'look like' the rest of the university. It is dominated by older, white men who truly believe that they are best positioned to make decisions

Those somewhere on the middle ground are missing in action, often because they've been physically or verbally shouted out of the debate

on behalf of the academic community. They have had control over the academic project since forever and they do not like their authority to be threatened. I think that it is very important that other voices are raised, and through generations of dispossession and frustration, when those voices are finally raised loud enough to be heard, they might sound angry and aggressive.

"We need to learn ways to hear those voices even if they are being expressed in ways that don't sound polite. If there are things said that need to be disagreed with, there should always be space for counterpoints to be shared." ⊗

Natasha Joseph is a contributing editor to Index on Censorship. She is based in Johannesburg, South Africa

Japan's Madonna complex

46(01): 22/25 | DOI: 10.1177/0306422017703590

As a new documentary sheds light on the sexualisation of young Japanese girls, **Annemarie Luck** reveals how women find themselves trapped by conflicting and extreme sexual stereotypes

JOSHIRYOKU. **IN JAPANESE,** this word means "girl power". Except it also doesn't. Rather than referring to traits of assertiveness and independence, the term describes, partially, a woman who is well-groomed, a wonderful cook and conforms to Japan's love of *kawaii* (cute) culture. Scary Spice would not be described as having *joshiryoku*. Neither, for that matter, would Japanese feminist artist Megumi Igarashi.

This spring, Igarashi (aka Rokudenashiko or "Good for Nothing Girl") faces her final court trial for the obscenity charges she's been battling since 2014. Her crime? Creating 3D printed sculptures, including a full-sized kayak, in the shape of her vagina, and then selling the 3D data to fund her art project. Igarashi's case, which has seen her arrested and fined with her art confiscated, has received worldwide attention. It's a prime example – as she puts it in her manga →

LEFT: A girl dressed in a manga-style costume poses for photos at a comic-book fair in Tokyo

→ book entitled What is Obscenity? – of Japan's "really weird view of pussy".

"Weird view" is one way to describe the layers of contradictions found within Japan's attitude towards sexuality. And it's these contradictions that are having a negative effect on Japanese women's ability to speak freely about their sexuality.

On the one hand, their sexuality is exploited for commercial gains. Men openly frequent hostess bars; police turn a blind eye to soaplands (bathhouses offering sexual services); and erotic manga showing buxom, yet childlike, women posing suggestively is displayed in every convenience store. A recent BBC documentary revealed that the rape of young girls is even featured in manga.

On the other hand, when pop idols, TV *tarento* ("talents") and artists like Igarashi

Penis festivals, in which huge phalluses are paraded through the streets, are well known in Japan

attempt to own their sexuality in even the smallest ways, they are publicly shamed and often silenced.

"As long as something serves the male *Makoto* gaze, it's condoned," said Natsu Kawasaki from Tomorrow Girls Troop, an artist collective that fights against gender inequality. The group endures a constant backlash so it operates anonymously, wearing pink rabbit masks that are symbolic of how women in Japan identify with the rabbit in Japanese mythology: "smart but powerless".

Their most recent work includes campaigning for the government to speed up revisions to the sex crimes law, which hasn't been updated in 100 years and is often cited as a reason only 4% of sexual assault crimes are reported, and an exhibition in Tokyo this February to create awareness around the

issue of sexual violence. The biggest opposition they have received came in 2015 after they demanded the city of Shima rescind a municipal mascot, which was a sexualised manga portrayal of a female, teenage *ama* (pearl) diver. They were not against a ban on all depictions, but were against the municipality, an authoritative entity, essentially promoting the sexualization of underage girls. The mascot was scrapped.

"We received huge criticism from the *otaku* [anime 'nerd'] culture, who said we were infringing on their freedom of expression. The sexualisation of young girls is so normalised that they completely missed the point."

Herein lies a crucial issue. "People in positions of authority are steeped in sexism. Teachers and even parents are dismissive of sexual exploitation, to the point where massive problems, such as the groping of girls on trains, are swept under the rug. As a result, girls grow up learning not to speak out, because when they do, they are criticised.

"In Igarashi's case," Kawasaki continued, "she is simply using her body in the way she wants to, yet she is censored and labelled a 'self-proclaimed artist'. But when a male artist such as Aida Makoto does the same thing with female bodies, his work is put in museums and he is called a 'genius'."

Author and critic Damian Flanagan, who has written extensively on Japanese politics, art and society, told Index on Censorship magazine: "The craziest part of the Igarashi story was not just the hypocrisy and blatant sexism – penis festivals, in which huge phalluses are paraded through the streets, are well-known in Japan – but the fact that the Japanese bureaucrats are so ignorant of their own cultural history. Some of the most extraordinarily graphic, fantastic 'vagina art' you will ever see forms an important part of the erotic art works of the Edo period."

Similar contradictions crop up regularly in Japan's entertainment industry, in which women are expected to maintain the squeaky

clean, child-like *kawaii* image, "but at the same time [women] are expected to prance around seductively in bikinis and schoolgirl uniforms when performing for men," said Kawasaki. If ever they transgress their contractual boundaries, they face grave consequences. Pop star Masuda Yuka was forced to leave idol group AKB48 for spending the night at a man's house; idol Minami Minegishi shaved her head and apologised after she was caught with a boyfriend; and TV personality Becky lost all her contracts after her affair with married pop star Enon Kawatani was exposed. His image was untarnished.

"At its most positive, *kawaii* is part of the gentleness and refinement that defines Japanese culture," said Flanagan. "The problem comes when you stop feeling that women are willing participants of *kawaii* culture, but are instead suppressing their own identity in order to provide a child-like face to the world. Even commanding, independent Japanese women can feel stifled by social conservatism and the effects of *kawaii* culture."

One industry that perhaps has the ultimate power to change viewpoints is the manga world. Even though erotic manga is criticised for sexually exploiting women and young girls, it's a form of art that speaks to all Japanese people. Artist Keiko Takemiya has been using manga to break taboos since the 1970s, when she became one of the first women to controversially create *shoujo* (manga aimed at a female readership). She told Index on Censorship magazine: "By using the main protagonist in manga to show how women can express their strengths, readers can relate to the character and take what they've learnt into the real world."

What does Takemiya think of fellow manga feminist Megumi Igarashi? "She's a courageous woman for challenging a society that's trying to reject her," she said. "Men's sexual desires are intrinsically exploitative. Yet it's almost impossible for women to sexually exploit men. That's why the Megumi Igarashi incident came about. Both men and women have to fully understand this contrast before they can talk about how to resolve sexual discrimination issues. I wonder if men have the courage to do that?" ⊗

Annemarie Luck is editor-in-chief of Tokyo Weekender magazine in Tokyo, Japan

ABOVE: Two members of Tomorrow Girls Troop wear their "smart, but powerless" signature pink rabbit masks

Squeezed in the closet

46(01): 26/28 I DOI: 10.1177/0306422017703591

Gay men and women in China are keeping their sexuality secret because of family and state attitudes, says **Hannah Leung**

WHEN CHINESE GAY dating app Blued announced this year that it was receiving millions in investment from state-run newspaper the Beijing News, it was a sign of the demand in the gay dating scene. The app has 27 million users, notable in a country where many gay people fear being discriminated against and ostracised by their families. This fear is simultaneously perpetuated by the government's shaky and often wavering support for LGBT communities.

"I didn't go home for Chinese New Year," says 31-year old Wen Yuxiao. Born and raised in a small town in the province of Hubei in central China, Wen now lives in the USA, pursuing a master's degree. Instead of returning to China, Wen opted for a short holiday with his partner. While going home would have been feasible, the impending family pressure ultimately swayed him against making the trip.

"I'm not out to my parents and I don't think I'll ever be. I'm an only child and, as the only son, the burden is really all on me. Since graduating, it's been the same rotation of questions. It used to be why I wasn't dating and now it's jumped straight to why I'm not married. I can't tell them that I am in a relationship, because it's not with a woman," he said.

China's Lunar New Year is a week-long national holiday full of family reunions, traditions and plenty of food. It is also a fraught and highly pressurised time for anyone single over the age of 25, as questions of marriage and children inevitably surface. Many in the LGBT community, for whom a conventional union isn't an option, feel pressure to keep quiet about their identity when at home over the holiday. An industry of renting a partner has even developed in response.

Homosexuality was illegal in China until 1997 and, despite official legalisation, societal acceptance – and even recognition – has been slow, especially in smaller provinces. This has led many to negotiate their sexuality alongside familial expectations. For the older generation, nothing is more important than the nuclear family, a foundation around Confucianist values and filial duty. But the pressure is further compounded by the one-child policy, introduced in 1979: millennials from the single generation household bear the weight of carrying on the family name.

Ju Huang, a 34-year-old gay man from southern Guangxi province living in Hong Kong, is another who cannot anticipate coming out to his mother, especially as his father died four years ago. As an only child, he feels pressure to appease her.

CREDIT: Rebel Pepper

"I would never come out to my mum. Where I come from, the societal norm is to land a stable job, get married and have kids. These are your sole responsibilities," he said.

He spent this year's Lunar New Year dodging questions from relatives about his dating life. While he has considered telling his classmates – some of whom are more open-minded – he hesitates out of fear that word will get back to his mother.

"I don't care about my own reputation, but if it goes back to my family, they will worry and face scrutiny from others. I don't want this to circulate," he said.

Ju has hatched a plan he hopes will appease both sides: "I won't marry a woman, but I plan on getting a surrogate. I haven't worked out the details of how I will explain why to my mum, but I think she will be happy if I just had a child. This is something I'm planning on doing within the next four to five years," he said.

Cover marriages and surrogacy are common within the LGBT community. Damien Lu, founder and president of Clearinghouse for Chinese Gays and Lesbians, →

→ a non-profit, said he had seen a rise in these arrangements over the last two years.

"Many gays are looking for ways to have children, simply to give to their parents, without understanding the implications and responsibility beyond. While some parents may accept that their sons or daughters have same-sex attraction, they still expect them to follow the traditions of marriage and reproduction," he said.

He added that this often resulted in dire consequences, and he has seen cases of children caught in legal battles when couples break up, and children raised primarily by grandparents and distant parents.

There are positive developments, with players trying to shift such expectations for the LGBT community. In 2015, the group Parents, Family and Friends of Lesbians and

Ironically, the success of gay dating app Blued can be attributed in part to the ban of Grindr

Gays made a popular short video telling the story of a man struggling to come out to his family over the New Year holiday. The man is immediately rejected by his parents, only for them to relent later and ask him to come home. The footage contains commentary from parents who have accepted their LGBT children and who are urging others to do the same. Despite the optimistic ending the short film provides, societal and structural acceptance still have a long way to go.

In March last year, the government banned the popular gay-themed online drama Addiction from being streamed on domestic platforms, three episodes short of completion. The show, which followed teenage boys in their coming-of-age sexualities, ended up airing the remaining episodes on YouTube, which is blocked in China, as are sites such as Facebook, Instagram and

Twitter. The ban was imposed by the State Administration of Press, Publication, Radio, Film and Television under the premise that it was not adhering to new regulations.

"From an art and culture perspective, there was no reason why this show should have been cancelled, as it was not profane. It was simply because the government didn't want to be seen as promoting gay values. And this comes at the expense of limiting the amount of gay-produced or gay-created art," said Lu, citing the case of filmmaker Fan Popo, whose documentary Mama Rainbow was taken off websites without a reason being given.

This tightening grip has been under way since current President Xi Jinping came into power. Xi's "anti-corruption" campaign has come at the expense of marginalised civil rights groups. Under his rule, netizens who congregated over Sina Weibo (a service similar to Twitter) have migrated to the more closed platform WeChat, where messages are visible only to an immediate circle of followers, and thus exempt from potential public ire. Ironically, the success of Blued can be attributed in part to the ban in China of another gay dating app, Grindr, alongside a slew of social media platforms with the ability to gather an international – and largely unmonitored – crowd. This is reflective of a shifting governmental stance on LGBT issues in China, being complicit and then suddenly restrictive, forcing communities to find ways to adapt in unstable environments.

For Wen, the ability to be fully himself can be done only overseas, a future he had planned since high school.

"I plan on staying in the USA for as long as possible. It might seem like a form of escapism, but at least this way my parents have less pressure from their friends about why I've made no plans for marriage. I can use the excuse of being overseas," he said. ⊗

Hannah Leung is a freelance journalist, based in Hong Kong

Degrees of separation

46(01): 29/33 I DOI: 10.1177/0306422017703607

As freedom of expression advocates worry about flashes of violence at US universities, **Jan Fox** reports on the growth of bias response teams, which encourage students to report on each other and their lecturers

HUNDREDS OF UNITS urging students to report on other students and lecturers they perceive as being biased have opened on US university campuses in the latest threat to free speech.

In its recently published national survey, the Foundation for Individual Rights in Education concluded that these units posed a growing threat. Bias referral teams suggest students should make reports to them when they perceive someone's speech is "biased". FIRE's survey identified 232 public and private colleges and universities that maintain these units, with a reach of an estimated 2.8 million students.

So what is "biased" speech? Joe Cohn, FIRE's legislative and policy director, said: "It's very vague. That's the problem – it makes students and [staff] afraid to say anything at all, lest it be perceived as biased." →

ABOVE: Demonstrators protest a visit by Corey Lewandowski, President Donald Trump's former campaign manager, at the University of Chicago in February 2017

||||||||||||||||||||||||||||||||||||||||||||||||||||||||||||||||||||||||||||||||||||||||||||||||||||||

#FREESPEECHHISTORY

UC Berkeley became a flashpoint for debate around freedom of expression when a campus protest against the visit of alt-right commentator Milo Yiannopoulos turned violent and saw his speech cancelled.

The location for such a protest against speech was ironic – the very same Sproul Hall on whose steps they were gathered was at the centre of the 1964 Free Speech Movement, a significant event at the university and in the story of civil rights and student politics in the 1960s.

At the start of the 1964-65 academic year, many UC Berkeley students, who had spent the summer on voter registration programmes and travelling with Freedom Riders in the south, were outraged by campus rules that banned them from soliciting support for political action. When a young man named Jack Weinberg was arrested for distributing civil rights literature in Sproul Plaza and thrown into a police car, thousands of students sat down around the car, preventing it from moving. Weinberg later described the sit-in as "an explosion of ideas". One after another, people climbed on top of the car to speak, about politics, philosophy and constitutional liberty. As they spoke the crowd grew and Weinberg's arrest was prevented for 32 hours.

The ban was lifted after a sit-in at Sproul Hall, the administrative building, in December 1964. Mario Savio gave a famous speech on the building's steps and then led around 2,000 people in occupying the building overnight. Eventually 773 were arrested as the building was cleared by police, but the point had been made. The faculty voted to repeal the rules and the freedom of speech movement, from the Young Socialists to the Young Republicans, won.

Kieran Etoria-King

→ The bias response teams are just the latest in a series of squeezes on academic freedom. When protest fires burned and windows were smashed on the campus of UC Berkeley recently, it only further stoked the debate as to whether the right to free

You are so lucky in America to have the right to free speech, and I hope you don't lose it

speech enshrined in the First Amendment of the US Constitution was under greater threat on campuses – the very places designed to promote thoughtful dialogue and engage a diversity of ideas – than almost anywhere else in the country.

Freedom of expression is being squeezed between ideas designed to protect students – such as safe spaces and trigger warnings – and protests, recently violent, by those wishing to shut down any ideas they don't want to hear. Between those who don't want to speak about uncomfortable issues and those who don't want to listen, is meaningful dialogue increasingly out the window?

It's a resounding yes from FIRE. Cohn said: "We are seeing student demand for freedom from speech rather than freedom of speech. We are turning off our critical thinking skills on campuses when the university should be the quintessential marketplace for ideas. Learning should sometimes be uncomfortable."

There has been much talk about "safe spaces" impacting freedom of expression. What began as a place where traumatised students might talk about experiences of sexual assault, racism and harassment, has ballooned to include many other topics, as well as student demands for segregated housing and dining (both CalState LA and UC Davis have segregated housing).

Cohn is not against safe spaces on an individual basis when a traumatised student might need one, but he is against the idea that an entire campus should be a safe space. He supports recent model legislation from Arizona-based think tank the Goldwater Institute that calls for the scrapping of safe spaces and free speech zones because, it says, both are eroding free speech. Campus Free Speech: A Legislative Proposal includes a lengthy report explaining the reason behind these calls and will be put to legislators and the public across the USA.

"Unequivocally, the calls for censorship on campus – and we get reports of them all day, every day at FIRE – are deeply troubling, so we are thrilled to see more people grappling with censorship and we welcome the Goldwater bill as a hopeful volley into this arena," said Cohn.

Whether the legislation has real bite is yet to be determined, and what Cohn calls a "volley" may be more a warning shot across the bow.

Free speech can also be shut down by students using the formal disinvitation process, through which they can challenge a speaker invited to the university to whom they object. More than 40 challenges were mounted in 2016, including to former Secretary of State Madeleine Albright at Scripps and Syracuse and to Vice President Joe Biden →

BELOW: A Donald Trump supporter who was attacked during protests at UC Berkeley in February 2017

ABOVE: Protesters rally against then Breitbart News editor Milo Yiannopoulos at UC Berkeley in February 2017

at Notre Dame. Previously, Condoleezza Rice, another former secretary of state, was challenged at Rutgers. But this year has seen a different type of challenge to an invited speaker.

Violence erupted at UC Berkeley in February as students protested against visiting speaker Milo Yiannopoulos, then an editor at the right-wing Breitbart News, who had been invited by the student Republican club. The protests prompted the university to cancel the event.

Louis Cheslaw, 21, a British student who recently returned home after spending a year at Berkeley, said he was disappointed at what had happened.

"I was upset as I saw Yiannopoulos's visit as an opportunity for a heavy but peaceful protest. He's a despicable man but he's free to speak. This violence is just shutting down the debate. President Obama said the best way to debate issues is to engage over your differences, and I agree."

Fellow Berkeley student Arielle Swedback, 20, is a senior staffer on the college newspaper the Daily Californian. "It's not the first time Berkeley has seen protest," she said. "You've only got to look at the 1950s and 1960s here, and in the Bay Area generally

and Oakland in particular, to know that and so, in one way, I don't see why anyone is surprised that the Yiannopoulos event resulted in this incident."

In 2015, Berkeley students shouted down a debate on the value of public education between Chancellor Nicholas Dirks and Executive Vice Chancellor and Provost Claude Steele. The protesting students wanted to raise awareness about certain issues on campus, including the size of Dirks' salary.

"I feel that this and many current protests are less about shutting down the debate around specific speakers and more about attracting attention to very real problems ranging across the political spectrum," said Swedback.

Last year's presidential election further narrowed campus debate. Post-election, anti-Donald Trump students held candlelit vigils and had counselling sessions on campus, while pro-Trump students demanded their own safe spaces and counselling as they felt afraid to speak out in support of the new president. The safe space appears to have become a place to avoid talking about almost everything, it seems.

Trigger warnings, designed to be given by teaching staff to students before they address sensitive topics in class, have also been in the spotlight. Oberlin College in Ohio climbed down from its expansive list in 2014 following significant pushback from academics, said Hans-Joerg Tiede, associate secretary of the department of academic freedom, tenure and governance at the American Association of University Professors.

"Since then we haven't gotten a lot of reports about trigger warnings," said Tiede. "Our main concern is about them being mandated, which is what Oberlin tried to do. But we were equally concerned at the statement put out by the University of Chicago last year saying it would not support any trigger warnings. Trigger warnings in some cases are perfectly acceptable but [colleges] should make that judgment and they should be on a case-by-case basis.

"The other problem with trigger warnings is that with a long list like Oberlin's was, you are worried you might miss something, and that can lead to self-censorship, which is another threat to freedom of expression on campus."

Dr Gad Saad, a Cornell alumnus and visiting professor at Dartmouth and UC Irvine, said: "Life is your trigger warning!" Saad, who also teaches at Concordia University, Montreal, is a self-confessed "academic warrior". He has his own YouTube channel, appears on talk shows to defend his views on freedom of expression and is organising a freedom summit in Canada.

When he was 11, he fled the Lebanese civil war during the 1970s with his family and settled in Canada. His experience helped make him a vocal supporter of free speech.

"People are castrated," said Saad. "They don't say anything harsh out of fear. I know fear – I've lived with death patrols coming to get you. Academics need to be warriors and stand up for freedom of expression. The pursuit of truth is greater than careerist issues."

Saad is against violence and hate speech but everything else, he said, is "up for grabs".

"Students are not committed to intellectual engagement – they are 'coddled'. Yes, if a student comes to me privately with an issue of sensitivity, of course I will listen, of course I will pay attention to their needs, but just saying 'don't offend me' is a type of lunacy."

Saudi Arabian law and human rights graduate Taghreed Haddadi gained her degree in California last year and has first-hand experience of censorship. "In Saudi Arabia, women are not free to express themselves and, more depressingly, in many cases they don't have the mental freedom to want to do so," she said. She added that people in the USA are lucky to have free speech still.

Similarly, Matt Mieskoski, who teaches at UC Irvine, said he'd never had "any blow-back" from subject matter he'd taught or language he used. He also sees the term "generation snowflake" as a misnomer.

Academics need to be warriors and stand up for freedom of expression

"It's the biggest myth there is. You've only got to look at how young people are standing up to what Trump is saying. The people who call others snowflakes get just as upset about the same things themselves."

The year ahead carries concerns for AAUP's Tiede. He said: "We are very concerned about the impact of the Trump administration in general on higher education and so I think there is a chance that we will see more violent protests this year. Violence should, of course, be condemned but when the president threatens to cut federal funds to Berkeley [as he did in a tweet after the unrest], I think there is reason to be very concerned about the future for freedom of expression." ⊗

Jan Fox is a contributing editor to Index on Censorship magazine, based in Los Angeles, USA

Dying to tell a story

46(01): 34/36 | DOI: 10.1177/0306422017703608

Writers in Bangladesh are facing pressure to shut up from Islamic extremists as well as government authorities, writes a director of Dhaka Lit Fest **Sadaf Saaz**

AHIGH-END CAFE IN an upmarket hotel in Dhaka is packed with people having morning meetings and going about their day as normal. It's a notable change from a few months ago when a terrorist attack in the summer on a similar cafe left 20 dead and punters stayed away from public spaces.

The return to normality however is relative, as Ahmad Mostofa Kamal explains over coffee. The award-winning writer is still under death threat from extremists.

"I always have that feeling of looking over my shoulder. I can never relax. Even today when I entered the building, I looked around to check if I was being followed," he told Index on Censorship magazine.

For writers this is not just paranoia. Bangladesh has seen a series of fatal attacks since 2013 against writers, publishers and bloggers. In 2015 a hit list of 84 names was circulated on the internet by Ansarullah Bangla Team, commonly known as Ansar Bangla, which is a militant group with links to al-Qaeda. Many of those on their hit list were labelled "secular bloggers" because of their atheist views and nine from the list have since been killed.

Ansar Bangla is thought to be one of the most active terror groups in Bangladesh and has been officially banned by the government.

According to blogger Arif Jebtik, who has also found himself under threat, "the fatal attacks have resulted in self-censoring, even among those who are not directly threatened." He reports how websites and blogs have closed down and many bloggers have left Bangladesh and haven't started writing again.

"Those like me who are here do not feel it is worth the risk. What if my son loses his father? Being under threat changes your life," Jebtik told Index.

Fighting for the right to express oneself has been at the core of Bangladesh's struggle for national identity. The constitution is based on secular and democratic principles,

with every citizen having the right to "freedom of speech and expression", albeit "subject to any reasonable restrictions".

But the ability to speak and write freely and without fear, which has enabled a rich and diverse literature and culture to flourish over centuries, is now under threat, not only from extremists but also from the government.

While the government was fast to take strong measures against militants after the terrorism attack at the cafe in the summer, they have been slow to ensure justice and to publicly condemn the killings of writers and minorities.

Indeed the government has actually placed the onus on writers to avoid writing

The government has actually placed the onus on writers to avoid writing anything 'objectionable' about religion

anything "objectionable" about religion. The ruling Awami League has called for writers to halt religious criticism and is using the law as their weapon. Prosecutors have brought charges against writers under the wide-ranging Section 57 of the Information and Communications Technology Act 2006 (amended in 2013), which makes peaceful expression a potential criminal act. The act can be used to prosecute anyone who publishes anything on or offline that hurts "religious sentiment" or prejudices the "image of the state".

Last year, for instance, during the country's largest book fair, Ekushey Boi Mela, held annually in February to celebrate International Mother Language Day, Shamsuzzoha Manik was arrested for publishing a book called Islam Bitorko (Debate on Islam). The book is now out of circulation, but Manik remains in jail a year later. →

CREDIT: Andrew Biraj/Reuters

OPPOSITE: More than 500,000 people gathered in Dhaka on 6 April 2013. Chants of "hang the atheist bloggers" were reportedly heard

→ At this year's book fair, the authorities warned against publishing and selling books that hurt "religious sentiment" and police vigilantly surveyed books stalls for any "offensive" material.

What is seen in some quarters as government pandering to the Islamic lobby in the country has also reached schools. Works by Hindu, Sufi and Christian writers, considered stalwarts of Bengali literature, like the great poet Michael Madhusudan Dutt, have been removed by the education department from primary and secondary school text books.

But censorship in Bangladesh is going further. Legislation like Section 57 has been used to censor critics of the government. For example, Section 57 has been invoked against those who have questioned facts about the 1971 war.

Campaigner Mithun Chakma, an or-

Being silent is not going to help. There are witty, satirical or subtle ways to say the same thing

ganiser for the United People's Democratic Front, a small political party from the Chittagong Hill Tracts in south-east Bangladesh, was arrested last July for publishing a blog where he accused a named army officer of abducting the indigenous rights campaigner and feminist Kalpana Chakma in 1996. He also claimed the army had embarked on a "massive cover-up campaign" after her disappearance. Chakma spent three months in jail without formal charges ever being filed against him. He is now on bail.

The draft Digital Security Act 2016 proposes to do away with the contentious Section 57, but there are fears that the new law on cybersecurity may limit freedom of expression even more. Its draconian clauses have been widely condemned by free speech groups; they include life sentences for spreading false information about the 1971 war or about the founder of Bangladesh, seven years for disturbing public order and two years for defamation or harming religious sensibilities.

Despite the squeeze from all sides, individuals are finding ways to write and express themselves, albeit carefully.

Reducing social media presence has been a strategy taken by Kamal, a way to be less in the limelight and therefore actually more free. "I have reduced writing on Facebook. Social media can be very immediate and reactive. I am committed not to compromise on my fiction and to remain in Bangladesh."

Mahrukh Mohiuddin of University Press Limited, a top Bangladeshi publisher, said: "The challenge is to find the right balance. Being silent is not going to help. There are witty, satirical or subtle ways to say the same thing. Often great writing comes out under difficult circumstances. Some writers are very good about saying what they want to say, even or especially in this present situation."

Fortunately there are still organisations willing to offer platforms to writers. The Dhaka Lit Fest is one such example. This year the Bangladesh government was a partner and provided full security. They did not try to exercise editorial control. The festival attracted an audience of 24,000 and took on controversial topics, including more than one packed session on freedom of expression. The government, in this instance, seemed keen to prove to the outside world that Bangladesh still has spaces for freedom of thought and expression.

Initiatives, personal and collective, reaffirm the importance of continuing to strive for these spaces, before they erode away even more. ⊗

Sadaf Saaz is a poet, writer, and the producer and a director of Dhaka Lit Fest

Trouble in paradise

46(01): 37/38 I DOI: 10.1177/0306422017703609

Independent journalists are being detained and prosecuted in the Maldives. **Zaheena Rasheed** investigates how a clampdown on press freedom is linked to its lucrative tourist trade

TWO JOURNALISTS FROM newspaper Maldives Independent were taken into "protective custody" by the government this spring. Their arrest came after they travelled to the Faafu Atoll ahead of a visit by Saudi Arabia's King Salman bin Abdulaziz, who was due to sign a controversial $10 billion investment deal to transform the atoll into a tourist super-resort.

These arrests are the latest in a series of crackdowns on the media by the government, which does not like opposition to its plans for massive tourism development, or any exposure of corruption that might tarnish its image.

Ismail Rasheed, former editor of Channel News Maldives, was made to close the website last June. "What I can say is that the pressure came right from the top," he said. "I was told we had no choice but to take it offline." →

ABOVE: President Abdulla Yameen before his inauguration in 2013

→ The final straw for the website, known for its exposés of abuses of human rights, was a series of articles alleging corruption by Maldives President Abdulla Yameen's wife.

CNM is not the only news outlet to suffer this fate over the past year. The Maldives' oldest newspaper, Haveeru, was also forced to shut last April. Journalists, who remained defiant despite death threats, murder attempts and the disappearance of a colleague, now opt for self-censorship because of the threat of jail under a new defamation law.

It was not always that way. The press flourished under former President Mohamed Nasheed, who ended 30 years of authoritarian rule in 2008. Until the mid 2000s, the main source of news was state television and radio, and three dailies owned by cabinet ministers. By 2012, there were at least six private television channels and an array of online media, most of which were controlled by politicians or tourism tycoons. But as one editor puts it, if you wanted to find out a specific perspective, it was available. Things changed when Nasheed was ousted and Yameen assumed office in 2013.

"What we saw was an increase in attacks on journalists and a policy by regime officials to buy out independent media," said Ismail Naseer, a former editor at Haveeru, which was shut after more than 30 years in print when a court split the paper's ownership. Prior to its closure, the paper lost five of its most senior and promising journalists when Yameen's right-hand man, Ahmed Adeeb, offered them cash to set up a rival news outlet.

At opposition-aligned Raajje TV it was a similar story. Half of the station's newsroom quit in 2014 to set up a new television channel, also funded by Adeeb. At the time the station was reeling from an arson attack that had destroyed its headquarters.

Under Yameen, state-owned enterprises have also begun pulling out advertising from independent media. Editors say state companies regularly threaten to terminate contracts over critical articles.

When news from the Maldives made global headlines, the country's tourism bosses, many of whom sit in parliament, worried that coverage, including of high levels of theft from state coffers, might deter tourists.

The tourism minister has hired seven public relations firms in China, Germany, the UK, India, France, South Korea and the USA to counter what he called misinformation that has tarnished the Maldives' reputation.

Yameen, who is seeking re-election in 2018, has also restricted the foreign press' access to the country.

Most irksome to the government was coverage of Islamic extremism by international media: in 2015, a four-member TV crew with German broadcaster ARD was deported and slapped with a 10-year ban for filming without a permit. Police also closely monitor foreigners visiting inhabited islands or asking too many questions.

JJ Robinson, a journalist who worked in the Maldives for four years, explained why the government was so sensitive about negative coverage, which has a substantial impact on tourism, "although not directly by discouraging audiences from visiting".

He said: "Rather, these reports contribute to travel advisories and insurance company risk assessors, which in turn have a significant influence on the large package holiday companies responsible for most of the tourism arrivals."

Robinson warned the policy would only backfire in the long run. "Hanging up a 'nothing to see here' sign is a great way to bring a flock of suspicious reporters disguised as tourists," he said.

The press is not about to give up. The team behind CNM have now set up Voice of the Free Press. "What else can we do? We have a social responsibility," said Rasheed, now the editor of VFP. "The future looks bleak. But we have seen worse." ⊗

Zaheena Rasheed is a former journalist at Maldives Independent, who is now at Al Jazeera

Your cover is shown

46(01): 39/41 | DOI: 10.1177/0306422017703610

As a new law presses New York's police to make public their rules on surveillance and encryption services come under fire, **Mark Frary** looks at threats to our ability to choose anonymity

THE ANONYMITY OF the crowd emboldens us to do what we otherwise might not. A 1969 study by US psychologist Philip Zimbardo found that "punishment" meted out to subjects by ordinary people was twice as harsh when the subjects' bodies and faces were covered and they were addressed as a group rather than as individuals.

While Zimbardo's research showed how anonymity makes us more aggressive (see social media any day of the week), the anonymity of the crowd also offers a cloak of invisibility to the weak and oppressed: the whistleblowers and political activists who risk their livelihoods and their lives to express opinions or facts that are inconvenient to those in power.

The importance of being able to remain anonymous online cannot be understated. In the early days of the Syrian revolution, President Bashar al-Assad was accused of using teams to monitor the online videos of anti-government protests in order to identify and arrest those who had taken part. As a result, YouTube has now introduced a custom blurring tool.

And in just the last few weeks legislation has been introduced that would make public the rules and techniques the New York City Police Department use for surveillance. The New York Civil Liberties Union said of the new measure: "For too long the NYPD has been using technology that spies on cell phones, sees through buildings and follows your car under a shroud of secrecy, and the bill is a significant step out of the dark ages."

With operational measures like these and with the British Home Secretary calling for access to encrypted Whatsapp messages, the anonymity the internet affords its 3.5 billion users is under serious threat. Anonymity is being squeezed by two factors that threaten not just to lift the cloak of invisibility but to tear it off completely. All individuals, and not just journalists, activists and freedom fighters, are now at risk of having all their interactions with phone networks and the internet captured and analysed.

The problem is that laws are being enacted that legitimise mass surveillance, while at the same time the speed of technological advance has made the possibility of analysing every single communication for its content a reality.

On 30 December 2016, the UK's Investigatory Powers Act came into force. The act explicitly authorises bulk interception and retention of both metadata and the content of electronic communications within the UK and overseas.

Edward Snowden's revelations about the UK Government Communications Headquarters' activities may have been embarrassing for the government, but far from scaling back these activities, the IPA embeds them into British law. →

→ Ian Walden, professor of information and communications law at Queen Mary, University of London, says that existing legislation was already being used to justify mass surveillance and the IPA has just made it explicit.

"The Intelligence Services Act 1994 has provision for property interference. What we didn't realise was that property interference extended all the way to hacking into systems," Walden told Index.

When the Snowden revelations were made public, the UK government was "between a rock and a hard place", he said. "They had to avow these practices and then had to redesign the legal framework to make sure it was resistant to legal challenge.

"Yet this may have unintended consequences elsewhere in the world. That avowal has the potential to legitimise everybody else to do it."

However, because of safeguards built into the act, Walden believes that the legislation, as a model for other countries, may be no bad thing.

"In many Commonwealth countries, the rule of law is much less robust and the

Although the scale of Tempora is breathtaking, no surveillance system currently known about can intercept and analyse all traffic on the internet and through telephone networks

practices of intelligence and law enforcement services are much less desirable [than in the UK]. If those countries take the oversight and the judicial review mechanisms from IPA then that is a good thing," he said.

The other big pressure on freedom of expression is advanced technology, specifically the ability to store and crunch large volumes of data, including the large amounts of data that pass through communications networks around the world.

Moore's Law – Intel founder Gordon Moore's projection in 1965 that computing power doubles every two years – has often been challenged, but it has held more or less consistently since he first stated it. And as computing power has grown, the cost of storage has also tumbled.

It is this that has enabled intelligence agencies around the world to start analysing signals intelligence on a massive scale through systems such as Prism and Tempora.

According to Snowden's leaked documents, Tempora "uses over 1,000 machines to process and make available to analysts more than 40 billion pieces of content a day". The system works by physically intercepting traffic on fibre-optic cables entering the UK. Tempora stores intercepted data for three days. It stores metadata, which is essentially the category labels that describe the underlying data, for 30 days.

Although the scale of Tempora is breathtaking, no surveillance system currently known about can intercept and analyse all traffic on the internet and through telephone networks.

The crucial point, though, is that GCHQ and other intelligence agencies do not need to look at everything. Streamed video like Netflix, for instance, which represents a large and growing portion of internet traffic is removed by Tempora and other systems from its analyses.

Advances in artificial intelligence also promise to help crunch data more effectively and GCHQ is actively courting start-ups through its GCHQ Cyber Accelerator programme, in partnership with the UK government and telecoms giant Telefonica. One of the first to win funding is StatusToday, a company that has developed an artificial intelligence-powered insights platform to analyse metadata.

In its 2016 report The Global Surveillance

Industry, Privacy International said, "The ability to monitor the communications of entire groups and nations on a mass scale is now a technical reality, posing new and substantially more grave human rights issues."

This surveillance is being carried out by agencies such as the NSA and GCHQ, but the involvement of the private sector cannot be ignored. A Bloomberg report estimated 70% of the 2013 US intelligence budget was spent with private companies. The Privacy International report investigated 528 of these surveillance technology providers and found that the USA and UK are the leading countries where such technologies are developed.

While a degree of anonymity still exists in the UK and USA, among others, it is not certain how long this will remain the case. Elsewhere in the world, states act with impunity and it is technology companies from those two countries that enable them. The anonymity of the crowd may well be dead. ⊗

Mark Frary is a regular contributor to The Times and Sunday Times. His latest book on cryptology, Codes, is due out later this year

46(01): 42/43 | DOI: 10.1177/0306422017703611

Rowson

MARTIN
ROWSON is a
cartoonist for
The Guardian
and the author
of various
books, includ-
ing Coalition
Book (2014),
a collection of
cartoons about
the UK's years
under a coalition
government

Composing battle lines

46(01): 44/47 | DOI: 10.1177/0306422017703613

South Korean entertainment websites are having to be extra careful about which music and films they broadcast to China as they tiptoe around rising political tension, writes **Steven Borowiec**

AS CHOI IL-JI explains how he curates websites featuring the latest in South Korean entertainment for Chinese audiences, his tone is equal parts excitement and anxiety. China has a strong appetite for South Korean music, films and fashion, but Choi operates in a fragile space where strong audience demand is tempered by strained diplomatic ties.

Korean entertainment has strong appeal across the East China Sea partly because Chinese viewers see a bit of themselves and their own country in the content, albeit a wealthier and more modern version of them. And with plotlines that revolve safely around tame love stories with minimal sexual content, Korean programmes often tend to sail past Chinese censors without much fuss, unlike comparatively raunchy fare from the USA. However this popularity can be used as a negotiating weapon by the Chinese authorities.

"Business people in China know they have a huge market that the rest of the world wants in on, so I think they feel like they can push other countries to play by their rules. If another country does something they don't like, they have the leverage to cut off access to their market," Choi said.

China is South Korea's largest trading partner. In early 2017, South Korean exports to China reached a high of $12 billion.

But Choi and other South Korean purveyors of pop culture have been struggling to adapt to political upheaval since Seoul agreed last year to the installation of the Terminal High-Altitude Area Defence, a US missile-defence system. In recent months it has become increasingly difficult for South Korean entertainers to access the Chinese market, and the reason for this, many speculate, is Chinese disapproval of the deal .

"China has made it clear that this is a kind of red-line issue for them. Going with THAAD meant that South Korea would take a hit in its ability to seek cooperation from China," said John Delury, a professor at Yonsei University in Seoul.

"It was like everything became disconnected. All of a sudden, so many projects were called off," Choi said in an interview at his office on the southern outskirts of Seoul. Choi's websites rely on revenue from Chinese advertisers, many of which have been caught in the diplomatic crossfire.

The conflict over THAAD, which is set to be deployed later this year, shows no sign of thawing. If there is a resolution, it could emerge in coming months when South

Koreans go to the polls to elect a new president following the decision in March to uphold the impeachment Park Geun-hye. Until a new president is elected, all major political decisions have been tabled.

"I think Chinese see Korea as somewhat more modern when it comes to fashion, plastic surgery and cosmetics. They look to Korea for what's hot before it gets to China," Delury said.

"To many Chinese, Korean culture is a more authentic kind of cool to aspire to. It's modern and Asian, and a way of being cool without mimicking what comes from the West," added Michael Hurt, an assistant professor of sociology at Hankuk University of Foreign Studies in Seoul.

It's not just Korea's fashion-forward image that appeals to Chinese audiences.

It was like everything became disconnected. All of a sudden, so many projects were called off

China and Korea have a shared history that goes back thousands of years as ancient Confucian civilisations. In modern times, both have found common ground opposing Japan's historical revisionism over "comfort women" and other World War II atrocities.

But the THAAD decision isn't the only factor squeezing Choi's room to operate freely in the Chinese market. When selecting the goods he promotes online, he must use content that Chinese audiences will find interesting, while being careful to filter out anything that might cause offence. His golden rule is "nothing political", but it is not always clear what amounts to "political". Chinese audiences can react sensitively to anything they perceive as disrespectful.

In August 2016, Chinese netizens responded with a flurry of criticism over →

OPPOSITE: South Korean pop star PSY performing during a charity football match in Shanghai

|||||||||||||||||||||||||||||||||||||||||||||||||||||||||||||||||||||||||||||||||||||||||||||||||||||

LITTLE BLACK BOOK

• South Korea's entertainment industry was plunged into a scandal of McCarthyist proportions during the winter, after a newspaper revealed that the government had compiled a blacklist of more than 10,000 artists.

• The daily Hankook Ilbo revealed in October 2016 that among the affected were high-profile personalities such as Park Chan-wook, the director of the hit movie Oldboy, and Booker Prize-winning author Han Kang. The blacklist was designed to prevent these artists from receiving state subsidies and private investment, and place them under state surveillance.

• The creation of the list was apparently ordered by the president's office in 2014, shortly after the MV Sewol ferry disaster, in which 304 people died. Many of the names on the list had been openly critical of the government's handling of the tragedy. The mayor of Busan, a member of President Park Geun-hye's party, had also tried to prevent the 2014 Busan Film Festival from screening a documentary named The Truth Shall Not Sink With Sewol, sparking huge protests and threats of boycott from industry professionals.

• The president is facing an impeachment trial on ever-increasing charges of corruption and abuse of power. Culture minister Cho Yoon-sun was arrested on 21 January, accused of abuse of authority and perjury for compiling the list.

• "The most serious problem is that authorities are trying to control our thoughts," filmmaker Ryoo Seung-wan told The Hollywood Reporter.

By Kieran Etoria-King

---

a South Korean television advert for US footwear brand K-Swiss. The ad depicted a South Korean actor winning a chess match against a plump Chinese man, who is later slapped by a woman during a dance battle. Many in China called the ad "humiliating", urging restrictions on Korean entertainers' access to China.

In 2015, Choi left a well-paid job as a television producer at KBS, a national broadcaster in South Korea, to take a risk on what he saw as an upcoming wave of commercial opportunity: China's growing appetite for cultural exports from South Korea.

Everything went well at first. Choi set up his online platform with carefully curated feeds of the latest South Korean music, films, fashion and celebrity news, and found local partners in China. But he would always carefully approach his business links with China.

"As a small country, we have to always respect our partners and follow global standards. We know we can't survive without outside partners," he said.

Mainland China's long-running dispute with Taiwan is another sensitive issue for Choi. In early 2016, Chou Tzu-yu, a teenage Taiwanese member of a South Korean girl group, was pressured to make a groveling public apology after she appeared on South Korean television waving a Taiwanese flag. In the controversy that ensued, Chou's management cancelled all her activities in China.

There are other cases of South Korean entertainers being frozen out of China, most without clear explanation. Last year, South Korean director Kim Ki-duk was denied a visa to shoot a film in China; after filming a TV series in China, actress Yoo In-na was informed her scenes had been cut; and an appearance by K-pop band Snuper on a Chinese show was scrapped at the last minute.

For Choi and others, there is a key difference in the extent to which they can manage factors limiting their freedom to operate. Choi can curate his offerings to avoid anything Chinese audiences may find offensive, but he has no power to negotiate his government's THAAD decision, nor Beijing's backlash against it. This means the recent turn of events is particularly damaging.

Nevertheless, Choi believes that the opportunities presented by the world's most populous country are enough motivation to keep him in business for the foreseeable future. "There's still more opportunity there than anywhere else. It's worth the struggle," he said. ⊗

Steven Borowiec is a freelance journalist based in Seoul, South Korea

BORDER CROSSING

JEMIMAH STEINFELD spoke to the man who helped smuggle out the only critical book about North Korea ever to have been written by an author still living in the country

North Korean author Bandi has no way of knowing his collection of short stories has been published, because no news from the West is ever likely to reach him.

Bandi, a pseudonym and a Korean word for firefly, is a state writer in North Korea. He put pen to paper in the late 1980s, just as the country was entering a particularly tumultuous and traumatic period. It was during this decade that a famine killed an estimated one million people, which also led to a rise in defections.

The Accusation, which was published this Spring in the USA and the UK, is the only known work of fiction critical of the North Korean regime written by someone still living in the country. The collection of seven short stories is unique because it gives a fictional voice to a whole variety of people who live under the regime; and it is the latest piece of contraband to be brought across the 38th Parallel, the world's most heavily fortified border crossing that divides North and South Korea.

Index spoke to Do Hee-yun, who helped smuggle the text out of North Korea. He said that even now Bandi is not fully safe. "North Korea pays attention to these stories," he told Index. As yet he is not aware of any effort to trace the writer, though there's a possibility that the authorities might look for Bandi if the book attracts a lot of attention. To this end some details have been altered, and Do explains there are measures in place to protect Bandi.

The manuscript was completed in 1993. When one of Bandi's relatives told him she was defecting, he asked her to smuggle his collection of stories out of the country. And so the book's perilous journey began. It eventually landed in the hands of Do.

"There may be an imaginative sense for idolisation, but North Korean society never allows writing to be imaginative or creative in other social areas," said Do.

More than 28,000 North Koreans have defected to South Korea since the country was split. Of those many have gone on to write books and some have become bestsellers. There's a concern that, writing specifically for an audience that want to read "bad North Korea stories", authors might resort to hyperbole. This makes Bandi's book a different beast. ⊗

Jemimah Steinfeld is deputy editor of Index on Censorship magazine

IN FOCUS

MAIN: A man painted with the Indian flag attends an Independence Day celebration in the eastern city Bhubaneswar, 15 August 2016

We have no time for fear

46(01): 50/51 I DOI: 10.1177/0306422017703614

Canan Coşkun, a journalist at daily newspaper Cumhuriyet who faces two upcoming trials for her reporting, talks about her attitude to the dangers of life as a reporter in Turkey

EVERY TWO TO three weeks recently, I have seen off a colleague leaving the courthouse for prison or snatched a few moments with a deeply missed, and now detained, workmate in the shadow of the authorities. But we aren't afraid of this dungeon darkness because we journalists are only doing our jobs.

I have been a court reporter for Cumhuriyet since 2013, so I spend the large majority of my working life in the courts. We all have moments we cannot forget from our working lives. For me, one such day was 5 November 2016, the day when 10 of our writers and managers were arrested. I was waiting for the court's decision right behind the barrier in the court building, and the moment I heard the decision I felt a flush of pride for our 10 writers and managers, followed by anger and deep depression for my friends.

I felt proud because the fact that they had been arrested for their journalism had been mentioned in the court's decision. In listing examples of our reporting as the reason for the arrests, the judge took the government's insistence that "they were not arrested for their journalism" and threw it out of the window. I felt anger and sadness because we were sending our friends off to an indefinite spell of captivity. The police would not even allow us to say goodbye to our colleagues who were only 30 or 40 metres away behind a barrier. But among the many feelings I had, fear was not one of them. When the attacks on journalism are on this scale, fear becomes a luxury.

After our 10 colleagues were arrested, many journalists from around Europe began visiting our newspaper's offices. Our foreign counterparts wanted to hear about what had happened and how we felt, and they all had the same question: "Are you afraid?" From November onwards, arrests of journalists have continued at a regular pace. But just as on that day, my answer to that question today is short and sweet: "No!"

We are not afraid, because we are doing our work and we are concerned only with our work. We are not afraid, because we

ABOVE: Turkish journalist Canan Coşkun previously faced a trial for her reporting on allegations of judges receiving discounts on homes. She now faces two more charges

too feel as if we have been in Silivri prison with our colleagues for these long months. We are not afraid, because very little difference remains between being in and out of prison. We are not afraid, because the heads of our jailed colleagues are held high. We are not afraid, because Fethullah Gülen, the exiled cleric accused by the government of being behind last year's failed coup attempt, was not once our "partner in crime". We are not afraid, because the Cumhuriyet that governments of every era have tried to silence has only reported, is only reporting and will only report.

Ahmet Şık, a reporter at my newspaper, has been under formal arrest since December 2016. Back in 2011, along with former military chief of staff İlker Başbuğ and many soldiers, police, journalists and academics, he spent more than a year in prison in relation to the "Ergenekon" case. The accusation was that they were attempting to overthrow the government.

Şık is currently under arrest accused of conspiring with the Gülen movement. But Turkey's justice system is such that the case in which Şık was arrested in 2011 still continues, and this gave us a chance to see him in court on 15 February. I waited outside the courtroom doors and when they opened all I saw inside was a face smiling with hope: he was able to see his friends for the first time in months. Although Şık is a much more experienced journalist than I am, his desk in the office was close to mine and I missed him.

At that hearing, he summarised today's fight to carry out journalism under the state of emergency, saying: "The story of those who think they have power, and who use this power to persecute journalists is as long as journalism itself."

Last December, six journalists, including some of my friends, were held for 24 days in an inquiry into the hacking of minister Berat Albayrak's emails. (Albayrak is President Recep Tayyip Erdogan's son-in-law.) Three of these journalists were later formally arrested by the courts. During this time, detained journalist Mahir Kanaat became a father, but he was unable to see his child. Fellow detainee Tunca Öğreten was not given the right to send and receive letters, or see anyone except his close relatives. He had to propose to his girlfriend via his lawyers.

Recently, I listened to one of these journalists relate a memory from his time in court. Having had their faith in justice shaken, they instead turned to superstition

When the attacks on journalism are on this scale, fear becomes a luxury

in the courtroom in a bid to be set free. Metin Yoksu, a freed journalist, said three of them had sat close to the courtroom exit and had replaced their shoelaces – which had been taken from them – with laces they had made from bits of water bottles. The result: those who were freed were those who had sat near the exit door.

Trust in Turkey's justice system has fallen so far that we now rely on our superstitions. How depressing. ⊗

Read about Index's Turkey Uncensored project on indexoncensorship.org

Translated by John Butler

*Journalist **Canan Coşkun** is a court reporter at Cumhuriyet. She is currently charged with defaming Turkishness, the Republic of Turkey and the state's bodies and institutions in one of her articles. Her article covered the story of a truck full of weapons hidden under onions. The second charge is that she depicted the police who combat terrorism as a target, for a story about Turkish Kurds being arrested*

Reel-time news

DECODING THE NEWS

46(01): 52/65 I DOI: 10.1177/0306422017703615

Manipulating news and discrediting the media are techniques that have been used for more than a century. In this special section, Index's global reporting team brief the public on how to watch out for tricks and spot inaccurate coverage. Below, Index on Censorship editor **Rachael Jolley** introduces the special feature

FICTIONAL ANGLES, SPIN, propaganda and attempts to discredit the media, there's nothing new there. Scroll back to World War I and you'll find propaganda cartoons satirising both sides who were facing each other in the trenches, and trying to pump up public support for the war effort. If US President Donald Trump is worried about the "unbalanced" satirical approach he is receiving from the comedy show Saturday Night Live, he should know he is following in the footsteps of Napoleon who worried about James Gillray's caricatures of him as very short, while the vertically challenged French President Nicolas Sarkozy feared the pen of Le Monde's cartoonist Plantu.

When Trump cries "fake news" at coverage he doesn't like, he is adopting the tactics of Ecuadorean President Rafael Correa. Correa repeatedly called the media "his greatest enemy" and attacked journalists personally, to secure the media coverage he wanted.

As Piers Robinson, professor of political journalism at Sheffield University, said: "What we have with fake news, distorted information, manipulation communication or propaganda, whatever you want to call it, is nothing new."

Our approach to it, and the online tools we now have, are newer however, meaning we now have new ways to dig out angles that are spun, include lies or only half the story.

But sadly while the internet has brought us easy access to multitudes of sources, and the ability to watch news globally, it also appears to make us lazier as we glide past hundreds of stories on Twitter, Facebook and the digital world. We rarely stop to analyse why one might be better researched than another, whose journalism might stand up or has the whiff of reality about it.

As hungry consumers of the news we need to dial up our scepticism. Disappointingly, research from Stanford University across 12 US states found millennials were not sceptical about news, and less likely to be able to differentiate between a strong news source and a weak one. The report's authors were shocked at how unprepared students were in questioning an article's "facts" or the likely bias of a website.

And, according to Pew Research, 66% of US Facebook users say they use it as a news source, with only around a quarter clicking through on a link to read the whole story. Hardly a basis for making any decision.

At the same time, we are seeing the rise of techniques to target particular demographics with political advertising that looks like journalism. We need to arm ourselves with tools to unpick this new world of information.

A PICTURE SPARKS A THOUSAND STORIES

KAYA GENÇ dissects the use of shocking images and asks why the Turkish media didn't check them

Two days after last year's failed coup attempt in Turkey, one of the leading newspapers in the country, Sozcu, published an article with two shocking images purportedly showing anti-coup protesters cutting the throat of a soldier involved in the coup. "In the early hours of this morning the situation at the Bosphorus Bridge, which had been at the hands of coup plotters until last night, came to an end," the piece read. "The soldiers handed over their guns and surrendered. Meanwhile, images of one of the soldiers whose throat was cut spread over social media like an avalanche, and those who saw the image of the dead soldier suffered shock," it said.

These powerful images of a murdered uniformed youth proved influential for both sides of the political divide in Turkey: the ultra-conservative Akit newspaper was positive in its reporting of the lynching, celebrating the killing. The secularist OdaTV, meanwhile, made it clear that it was an appalling event and it was publishing the pictures as a means of protest.

Neither publication credited the images they had published in their extremely popular articles, which is unusual for a respectable publication. A careful reader could easily spot the lack of sources in the pieces too; there was no eyewitness account of the purported killing, nor was anyone interviewed about the event. In fact, the piece was written anonymously.

These signs suggested to the sceptical reader that the news probably came from someone who did not leave their desk to write the story, choosing instead to disseminate images they came across on social media and to not do their due diligence in terms of verifying the facts.

On 17 July, Istanbul's medical jurisprudence announced that, among the 99 dead bodies delivered to the morgue in Istanbul, there was no beheaded person. The office of Istanbul's chief prosecutor also denied the news, and it was declared that the news was fake.

A day later, Sozcu ran a lengthy commentary about how it prepared the article. Editors accepted that their article was based on rumours and images spread on social media. Numerous other websites had run the same news, their defence ran, so the responsibility for the fake news rested with all Turkish media. This made sense. Most of the pictures purportedly showing lynched soldiers were said to come from the Syrian civil war, though this too is unverifiable. Major newspapers used them, for different political purposes, to celebrate or condemn the treatment of putschist soldiers.

More worryingly, the story showed how false images can be used by both sides of Turkey's political divide to manipulate public opinion: sometimes lies can serve both progressives and conservatives.

Kaya Genç is a contributing editor for Index on Censorship magazine based in Istanbul, Turkey

X
46.01

DECODING THE NEWS

Homepage | China | World | Photos | Video | Special Reports   Saturday, Feb. 25, 2017

New China

Search

New China   **Top News**   **Latest News**   **Photos**   **Video**

Latest News ⏮⏭ Ten rising stars in Chinese squad at Winter Asiad

Alibaba's Jack Ma to fund education of 8-year-old look-alike

Source: Xinhua | 2016-11-14 16:29:37 | Editor: huaxia

"Mini Jack Ma" Fan Xiaoqin (web photo)

Jack Ma, China's second richest man, will fund the education of his eight-year-old doppelganger, according to a statement from e-commerce giant Alibaba released Sunday.

The boy, Fan Xiaoqin, earned the nickname "mini Jack Ma" when photos of him showing a striking resemblance to the Alibaba founder were posted online last year.

Ma was impressed with the look-alike.

Younger Jack Ma (Left) (web photo)

"At first glance, I thought it was a photo of me when I was little," he wrote in a post on Sina Weibo last year. "I thought I was looking into a mirror."

"The only difference between us is the way we fastened our buttons," he added.

The photos and video of little Fan, who lives in Yongfeng County in east China's Jiangxi Province, were originally taken and posted online by a fellow villager in the winter of 2014. The boy soon became a cyber-celebrity and his plight has moved many.

There's no direct quote in which Ma pledges to specifically support Fan, nor a quote from Fan or his family

The rest of the article uses rehashed information and images

56
INDEXONCENSORSHIP.ORG

|||||||||||||||||||||||||||||||||||||||||||||||||||||||||||||||||||||||||||||||||||||||||||||||

A CASE OF MISTAKEN PHILANTHROPY

JEMIMAH STEINFELD writes on the story of Jack Ma's doppelganger that went too far

Jack Ma is China's version of Mark Zuckerberg. The founder and executive chairman of successful e-commerce sites under the Alibaba Group, he's one of the wealthiest men in China. Articles about him and Alibaba are frequent. It's within this context that an incorrect story on Ma was taken as verbatim and spread widely.

The story, published in November 2016 across multiple sites at the same time, alleged that Ma would fund the education of eight-year-old Fan Xiaoquin, nicknamed "mini Ma" because of an uncanny resemblance to Ma when he was of a similar age. Fan gained notoriety earlier that year because of this. Then, as people remarked on the resemblance, they also remarked on the boy's unfavourable circumstances – he was incredibly poor and had ill parents. The story took a twist in November, when media, including mainstream media, reported that Ma had pledged to fund Fan's education.

Hints that the story was untrue were obvious from the outset. While superficially supporting his lookalike sounds like a nice gesture, it's a small one for such a wealthy man. People asked why he wouldn't support more children of a similar background (Fan has a brother, in fact). One person wrote on Weibo: "If the child does not look like Ma, then his tragic life will continue."

Despite the story drawing criticism along these lines, no one actually questioned the authenticity of the story itself. It wouldn't have taken long to realise it was baseless. The most obvious sign was the omission of any quote from Ma or from Alibaba Group. Most publications that ran the story listed no quotes at all. One of the few that did was news website New China – sponsored by state-run news agency Xinhua. Even then the quotes did not directly pertain to Ma funding Fan. New China also provided no link to where the comments came from.

Copying the comments into a search engine takes you to the source though – an article on major Chinese news site Sina, which contains a statement from Alibaba. In this statement, Alibaba remark on the poor condition of Fan and say they intend to address education amongst China's poor. But nowhere do they pledge to directly fund Fan. In fact, the very thing Ma was criticised for – only funding one child instead of many – is what this article pledges not to do.

It was not just the absence of any comments from Ma or his team that was suspicious; it was also the absence of any comments from Fan and his family. Media that ran the story had not confirmed its veracity with Ma or with Fan. Given that few linked to the original statement, it appeared that not many had looked at that either.

In fact, once past the initial claims about Ma funding Fan, most articles on it either end there or rehash information that was published from the initial story about Ma's doppelganger. As for the images, no new ones were used. These final points alone wouldn't indicate that the story was fabricated, but they do further highlight the dearth of new information, before getting into the inaccuracy of the story's lead.

Still, the story continued to spread, until someone from Ma's press team went on the record and denied the news, or lack thereof.

Jemimah Steinfeld is deputy editor of Index on Censorship magazine

NOT A LAUGHING MATTER

DUNCAN TUCKER digs out the clues that a story about clown killings in Mexico didn't stand up

Disinformation thrives in times of public anxiety. Soon after a series of reports on sinister clowns scaring the public in the USA in 2016, a story appeared in the Mexican press about clowns being beaten to death.

At the height of the clown hysteria, the little-known Mexican news site DenunciasMX reported that a group of youths in Ecatepec, a gritty suburb of Mexico City, had beaten two clowns to death in retaliation for intimidating passers-by. The article featured a low-resolution image of the slain clowns on a run-down street, with a crowd of onlookers gathered behind police tape.

To the trained eye, there were several telltale signs that the news was not genuine.

While many readers do not take the time to investigate the source of stories that appear on their Facebook newsfeeds, a quick glance at DenunciasMX's "Who are we?" page reveals that the site is co-run by social activists who are tired of being "tricked by the big media mafia". Serious news sources rarely use such language, and the admission that stories are partially authored by activists rather than by professionally-trained journalists immediately raises questions about their veracity.

The initial report was widely shared on social media and quickly reproduced by other minor news sites but, tellingly, it was not reported in any of Mexico's major newspapers – publications that are likely to have stricter criteria with regard to fact-checking.

Another sign that something was amiss was that the reports all used the vague phrase "according to witnesses", yet none had any direct quotes from bystanders or the authorities.

Yet another red flag was the fact that every news site used the same photograph, but the initial report did not provide attribution for the image. When in doubt, Google's reverse image search is a useful tool for checking the veracity of news stories that rely on photographic evidence. Right-clicking on the photograph and selecting "Search Google for Image" enables users to sift through every site where the picture is featured and filter the results by date to find out where and when it first appeared online.

In this case, the results showed that the image of the dead clowns first appeared online in May 2015, more than a year before the story appeared in the Mexican press. It was originally credited to José Rosales, a reporter for the Guatemalan news site Prensa Libre. The accompanying story, also written by Rosales, stated that the two clowns were shot dead in the Guatemalan town of Chimaltenango.

While most of the fake Mexican reports did not have bylines and contained very little detail, Rosales's report was much more specific, revealing the names, ages and origins of the victims, as well as the number of shell casings found at the crime scene. Instead of rehashing rumours or speculating why the clowns were targeted, the report simply stated that police were searching for the killers and were working to determine the motive.

As this case demonstrates, with a degree of scrutiny and the use of freely available tools, it is often easy to differentiate between genuine news and irresponsible clickbait.

Duncan Tucker is a regular correspondent for Index on Censorship magazine from Mexico

Info Noticias

Política   Policiaca   Salud   Insólito   Quienes somos   Contacto   Copyright   ▼   Search...

** » Policiaca » Mataron a 2 payasos que asustaban a niños y mujeres en Ecatepec

Mataron a 2 payasos que asustaban a niños y mujeres en Ecatepec

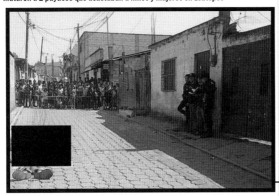

This site is little-known and run by people who describe themselves as activists against mainstream media

Ecatepec, Estado de México.- Aquí en el país azteca no nos andamos con bromitas: apenas entró la modita de que personas vestidas de payasos andan asustando a la gente, cuando en Ecatepec ya mataron a dos por jugarle al valiente.

Dos sujetos que vestían los trajes de bufones fueron encontrados sin vida en la colonia America Santa Clara, en Ecatepec, Estado de México la mañana del viernes.

Según dijeron los testigos, este par de sujetos estaban asustando a los transeúntes cuando fueron enfrentados por un grupo de jóvenes que –hartos de la bromita- les pusieron una furiosa tunda hasta matarlos.

En Ecatepunk no se andan con rodeos y pues 'se los cargó el payaso'.

Los hechos acontecieron cerca de las 2 de la madrugada y fue hasta el amanecer cuando los cuerpos fueron levantados por el Servicio Médico Forense (Semefo).

La modita de estos payasos viene de los Estados Unidos, donde es común ver que las personas salgan corriendo despavoridas. Sin embargo, aquí la gente ya no le tiene miedo ni a la muerte por lo que los se deberían de cuidar son los payasos.

The photo was taken a year before the event of the story purportedly took place

Escrito por: Diego Velázquez R.

 85.7K 899

ANTERIOR
Diputados compraron autos "debajo del agua", para rifarlos entre puros cuates

SIGUIENTE
La pintora que superó a Frida Kahlo, pero murió olvidada por todos

777 comentarios   Ordenar por: Los más antiguos ▼

 Añade un comentario...

 Monky Creazy · Universidad Michoacana de San Nicolás de Hidalgo
POR MAMONES Y PENDEJOS ...

PUBLICACIONES VIRALES

 Adolfo López Mateos escribió una carta "por si alguien se le ocurría vender la nación"
En 1960 Adolfo López Mateos envió una carta abierta a la nación, pensando que quizá en un futuro sus palabras iban a tener un eco. É... **1**

 Diputados aprobaron nueva ley para reducir un 50% el salario de un trabajador enfermo por cuestiones laborales
Ciudad de México.- Si usted creía que los Diputados trabajan por un México más igual e inclusivo, se equivoca. Nuestro país se encuent... **2**

 Peña Nieto autoriza bajar 2 centavos la gasolina para apoyar al pueblo, "yo si cumplo" dijo
2 centavos será un gran ahorro para el pueblo, dijo La Secretaría de Hacienda y Crédito Público informó este viernes que el precio ... **3**

The Awaze Tribune
Fearless News, Analysis & Investigative Reporting

HOME   WORLD ⌄   ELECTIONS ⌄   IMMIGRATION ⌄   MORE ⌄

Home › World › Asia › North Korean Ambassador to UN: "Stop Calling Eritrea the North Korea of...

World   Asia   Africa   Eritrea   Immigration

North Korean Ambassador to UN: "Stop Calling Eritrea the North Korea of Africa"

By **Editor** - June 27, 2016   👁 37248   💬 8

Language such as "senile idiot" attributed to a diplomat is a red herring

AFRICAN DICTATOR OF A SAD LITTLE NATION." AMBASSADOR SON SAID.

Ambassador Son further went on to compare the accomplishments of DPRK Premier Kim Sung-il versus that of Isaias Afwerki of Eritrea, who he kept referring to as "that senile idiot" through his briefing.

" THROUGH THE LEADERSHIP OF OUR GLORIOUS DEAR LEADER, THE DPRK IS A

Eritrea : Activist Implores Home Government to Introduce Mandatory Swimming Lessons

Eritrea   Editor   December 27, 2016   0

The Awaze Tribune
Fearless News, Analysis & Investigative Reporting

HOME   WORLD ⌄   ELECTIONS ⌄   IMMIGRATION ⌄   MORE ⌄

The About Us section is a complete spoof

Home › About

About

About The Awaze Tribune

The Awaze Tribune, hereafter shortened to AT, is the world's leading news website, offering highly praised, acclaimed and revered coverage of current events and news– AT staffers have won multiple Pulitzer prizes for their fearless, timely and insightful coverage of events and cover breaking news both in the international and national arenas.

From its founding in 32 A.D., AT has covered numerous newsworthy events– from the Baptism of Jesus Christ, to his cruxi-fiction, to the Birth of Prophet Mohammed(PBWH) and his famous Milk miracles, to the suicide of President Lincoln as well as the coverage of NASA's secret but successful space mission to the Sun. Awaze Tribune enjoys a 14 billion unique daily visits and is the only news website that employs over 1 million correspondents, editors, journalists, producers and janitors.

AT maintains by far, the most successful and highest standards of excellence in the world of journalism — which newspapers such as the New York Times or the Guardian can only aspire to equal. Our Style Manual is so secret and of the highest quality that, we are

FOLLOW US

f   0 Fans   LIKE

🐦   62,695 Followers   FOLLOW

▶   2,521 Subscribers   SUBSCRIBE

- Advertisement -

NOT NORTH KOREA

ABRAHAM T ZERE dissects the moment that Eritreans mistook saucy satire for real news

In recent years, the international media have dubbed Eritrea the "North Korea of Africa", due to their striking similarities as closed, repressive states that are blocked to international media. But when a satirical website run by exiled Eritrean journalists cleverly manipulated the simile, the site stoked a social media buzz among the Eritrean diaspora.

Awaze Tribune launched last June with three news stories, including "North Korean ambassador to UN: 'Stop calling Eritrea the North Korea of Africa'."

The story reported that the North Korean ambassador, Sin Son-ho, had complained it was insulting for his advanced, prosperous, nuclear-armed nation to be compared to Eritrea, with its "senile idiot leader" who "hasn't even been able to complete the Adi Halo dam".

With apparent little concern over its authenticity, Eritreans in the diaspora began widely sharing the news story, sparking a flurry of discussion on social media and quickly accumulating 36,600 hits.

The opposition camp shared it widely to underline the dismal incompetence of the Eritrean government. The pro-government camp countered by alleging that Ethiopia must have been involved behind the scenes.

The satirical nature of the website should have seemed obvious. The name of the site begins with "Awaze", a hot sauce common in Eritrean and Ethiopian cuisines. If readers were not alerted by the name, there were plenty of other pointers. For example, on the same day, two other "news" articles were posted: "Eritrea and South Sudan sign agreement to set an imaginary airline" and "Brexit vote signals Eritrea to go ahead with its long-planned referendum".

Although the website used the correct name and picture of the North Korean ambassador to the UN, his use of "senile idiot" and other equally inappropriate phrases should have betrayed the gag.

Recently, Eritrean President Isaias Afwerki has been spending time at Adi Halo, a dam construction site about an hour's drive from the capital, and he has opened a temporary office there. While this is widely known among Eritreans, it has not been covered internationally, so the fact that the story mentioned Adi Halo should also have raised questions of its authenticity with Eritreans. Instead, some readers were impressed by how closely the North Korean ambassador appeared to be following the development.

The website launched with no news items attributed to anyone other than "Editor", and even a cursory inspection should have revealed it was bogus. The About Us section is a clear joke, saying lines such as the site being founded in 32AD.

Satire is uncommon in Eritrea and most reports are taken seriously. So when a satirical story from Kenya claimed that Eritrea had declared polygamy mandatory, demanding that men have two wives, Eritrea's minister of information felt compelled to reply.

In recent years, Eritrea's tightly closed system has, not surprisingly, led people to be far less critical of news than they should be. This and the widely felt abhorrence of the regime makes Eritrean online platforms ready consumers of such satirical news.

*Journalist **Abraham T Zere** is originally from Eritrea and now lives in the USA. He is executive director of PEN Eritrea*

AND THAT'S A CUT

Journalist NATASHA JOSEPH spots the signs of fiction in a story about circumcision

The smartest tall tales contain at least a grain of truth. If they're too outlandish, all but the most gullible reader will see through the deceit. Celebrity death stories are a good example. In South Africa, dodgy "news" sites routinely kill off local luminaries like Desmond Tutu. The cleric is 85 years old and has battled ill health for years, so fake reports about his death are widely circulated.

This "grain of truth" rule lies at the heart of why the following headline was perhaps believed. The headline was "Men can now circumcise themselves at home, it is easy – says minister of health". Circumcision is a common practice among a number of African cultural groups. Medical circumcision is also on the rise. So it makes sense that South Africa's minister of health would be publicly discussing the issue of circumcision.

The country has also recently unveiled "DIY HIV testing kits" that allow people to check for HIV in their own homes. This is common knowledge, so casual or less canny readers might conflate the two procedures.

The reality is that most of us are casual readers, snacking quickly on short pieces and not having the time to engage fully with stories. New levels of engagement are required in a world heaving with information.

The most important step you can take in navigating this terrible new world is to adopt a healthy scepticism towards everything. Yes, it sounds exhausting, but the best journalists will tell you that it saves a lot of time to approach information with caution. My scepticism manifests as what I call my "bullshit detector". So how did my detector react to the "DIY circumcision" story?

It started ringing instantly thanks to the poor grammar evident in the headline and the body of the text. Most proper news websites still employ sub editors, so lousy spelling and grammar are early warning signals that you're dealing with a suspicious site.

The next thing to check is the sourcing: where did the minister make these comments? To whom? All this article tells us is that he was speaking "in Johannesburg". The dearth of detail should signal to tread with caution. If you've got the time, you might also Google some key search terms and see if anyone else reported on these alleged statements. Also, is there a journalist's name on the article? This one was credited to "author", which suggests that no real journalist was involved in production.

The article is accompanied by some graphic illustrations of a "DIY circumcision". If you can stomach it, study the pictures. They'll confirm what I immediately suspected upon reading the headline: this is a rather grisly example of false "news".

Finally, make sure you take a good look at the website that runs such an article. This one appeared on African News Updates.

That's a solid name for a news website, but two warning bells rang for me: the first bell was clanged by other articles, which ranged from the truth (with a sensational bent) to the utterly ridiculous. The second bell rang out of control when I spotted a tab marked "satire" along the top. Click on it and there's a rant ridiculing anyone who takes the site seriously. Like I needed any excuse to exit the site and go in search of real news.

Natasha Joseph is a contributing editor for Index on Censorship magazine and is based in Johannesburg, South Africa. She is also Africa education, science and technology editor at The Conversation

BREAKING NEWS Bafana Bafana to play with their own balls at home

AFRICAN NEWS UPDATES
What's Trending in Africa?

HOME NEWS POLITICS AFRICA FAITH SATIRE ABOUT US DISCLAIMER CONTACT US
SUBMIT ARTICLE

Home / Education / Health / News / Men can now circumcise themselves at home, it is easy- says minister of Health

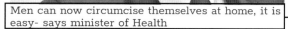

Men can now circumcise themselves at home, it is easy- says minister of Health

EDUCATION, HEALTH, NEWS — *21st December 2016, by news* 💬 Comments Off 👁 2515

Due to the huge number of uncircumcised men in South Africa and the limited resources our country has, the department of health has come up with a method for men to circumcise themselves at home.

The minister of health revealed this morning that people do not need to worry about going to hospitals for circumcision as there is an easier and cheaper method to do this.

Speaking to a group of journalists, Minister Aaron Motsoaledi this morning said, "We are doing everything in our power to fight against HIV and AIDS, uncircumcised men stand a huge chance of contracting the virus if they have unprotected sex. So, we encourage people to get circumcised. It is not a difficult thing to do, people can now even do it at home."

Here is the method below:

By using a small mirror (unless your manhood is very big), you can verify that your personal member does not have some extra, unwanted skin at the end.

For this procedure you will need *A kitchen knife, 12 cans of beer, a roll of paper towels, and your penis.*

DO-IT-YOURSELF CIRCUMCISION!
FOUR EASY STEPS!   **TRY AT HOME!**

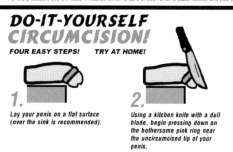

1. Lay your penis on a flat surface (over the sink is recommended).

2. Using a kitchen knife with a dull blade, begin pressing down on the bothersome pink ring near the uncircumcised tip of your penis.

3. Move the knife back and forth, applying liberal amounts of Crisco oil in the process. Stop when it cuts all the way through, or you hear a "popping" sound.

4. Immediately apply paper towels saturated with Crisco oil to the sacred wound. Wait seven days before returning to church.

©2001 landoverbaptist.org

WARNING! BEFORE YOU BEGIN:

The grammar is poor even in the headline

You don't need to be a doctor (or a health minister) to spot the problems here

CREDIT:Nic Bothma/AFP/Rex

GET THE TRICKS
OF THE TRADE

Veteran journalist RAYMOND JOSEPH explains how a handy new tool from South Africa can teach you core journalism skills to help you get to the truth

It's been more than 20 years since leading US journalist and journalism school teacher Melvin Mencher released his Reporter's Checklist and Notebook, a brilliant and simple tool that for years helped journalists in training.

Taking cues from Mencher's, there's now a new kid on the block designed for the digital age. Pocket Reporter is a free app that leads people through the newsgathering process – and it's making waves in South Africa, where it was launched in late 2016.

Mencher's consisted of a standard spiral-bound reporter's notebook, but also included tips and hints for young reporters and templates for a variety of stories, including a crime, a fire and a car crash. These listed the questions a journalist needed to ask.

Cape Town journalist Kanthan Pillay was introduced to Mencher's notebook when he spent a few months at the Harvard Business School and the Nieman Foundation in the USA. Pillay, who was involved in training young reporters at his newspaper, was inspired by it. Back in South Africa, he developed a website called Virtual Reporter.

"Mencher's notebook got me thinking about what we could do with it in South Africa," said Pillay. "I believed then that the next generation of reporters would not carry notebooks but would work online."

Picking up where Pillay left off, Pocket Reporter places the tips of Virtual Reporter into your mobile phone to help you uncover the information that the best journalists would dig out. Cape Town-based Code for South Africa re-engineered it in partnership with the Association of Independent Publishers, which represents independent community media.

It quickly gained traction among AIP's members. Their editors don't always have the time to brief reporters – who might be inexperienced journalists or untrained volunteers – before they go out on stories.

This latest iteration of the tool, in an age when any smartphone user can be a reporter, is aimed at more than just journalists. Ordinary people without journalism training often find themselves on the frontline of breaking news, not knowing what questions to ask or what to look out for.

Code4SA recently wrote code that makes it possible to translate the content into other languages besides English. Versions in Xhosa, one of South Africa's 11 national languages, and Portuguese are about to go live. They are also currently working on Afrikaans and Zulu translations, while people elsewhere are working on French and Spanish translations.

"We made the initial investment in developing Pocket Reporter and it has shown real world value. It is really gratifying to see how the project is now becoming community-driven," said Code4SA head Adi Eyal.

Editor Wara Fana, who publishes his Xhosa community paper Skawara News in South Africa's Eastern Cape province, said: "I am helping a collective in a remote area to launch their own publication, and Pocket Reporter has been invaluable in training them to report news accurately." His own journalists were using the tool and he said it had helped improve the quality of their reporting.

Cape Peninsula University of Technology journalism department lecturer Charles King is planning to incorporate Pocket Reporter into his curriculum for the news writing and online-media courses he teaches.

"What's also of interest to me is that there will soon be Afrikaans and Xhosa versions of

Ordinary people without journalism training often find themselves on the frontline of breaking news

the app, the first languages of many of our students," he said.

Once it has been downloaded from the Google Play store, the app offers a variety of story templates, covering accidents, fires, crimes, disasters, obituaries and protests.

The tool takes you through a series of questions to ensure you gather the correct information you need in an interview.

The information is typed into a box below each question. Once you have everything you need, you have the option of emailing the information to yourself or sending it directly to your editor or anyone else who might want it.

Your stories remain private, unless you choose to share them. Once you have emailed the story, you can delete it from your phone, leaving no trace of it.

Raymond Joseph *is former editor of Big Issue South Africa and regional editor of South Africa's Sunday Times. He is based in Cape Town and tweets @rayjoe*

Singing from the same hymn sheet

46(01): 66/68 | DOI: 10.1177/0306422017703616

The student who is being prosecuted for not standing up for the Indian national anthem talks to **Suhrith Parthasarathy** about freedom

WHEN SHREELA MANOHAR, 27, a law student in Chennai, India, spoke to Index on Censorship magazine, she was facing charges for failing to stand up and respect the Indian national anthem when it was played before the screening of a film at the Chennai International Film Festival. The law under which she was charged remains vague, and difficult to enforce. The lack of clarity is a result of a Supreme Court order, delivered in November last year, which made it compulsory for Indian cinemas to play the national anthem, and for those present in the halls to stand up and show their respect, despite the absence of any legislation demanding such rules. The order's consequences on free speech in India, as Manohar's predicament shows, have been enormous.

"It's a serious blow to my basic civil rights," Manohar told Index. "My mother and I were merely sitting down when the anthem was being played. We didn't stop anybody from singing it, nor did we in any way disrespect the anthem."

Manohar's apparent act of disobedience, though, piqued a small minority of fellow cinema-goers, who called the police. Manohar, her mother and Bejon K David, 21, a recent graduate, who had also refused to stand up for the anthem, were summoned to a police station, and a case was initiated against them under the 1971 Prevention of Insults to National Honour Act.

David, a resident of Kottayam, Kerala, had gone to Chennai to watch films at the festival. "The cops were a bit perplexed on how to deal with the situation," he told Index. "They weren't sure that a failure to stand up for the anthem was a crime, but they were ultimately convinced that if the Supreme Court mandated it then it must be a wrong for which we must be punished."

Section three of the 1971 legislation states that whoever intentionally prevents the singing of the national anthem or disturbs such singing by any assembly shall be punished with imprisonment for up to three years. The law, however, doesn't penalise a failure to stand up when the anthem is played. This diktat, which is new, flows from the Supreme Court's order, which legal experts say is a form of judicial censorship. The court's decision also comes at a time when the Indian government is just as concerned with enforcing perceived nationalistic values, often with little concern for the right to freedom of expression.

In India, the right to free speech and expression is guaranteed by a clause in the constitution. Another clause, however, permits

OPPOSITE:
Students salute the national flag during celebrations to mark Republic Day in Hyderabad on 26 January 2017

the state to make "reasonable restrictions" on the right to free speech in the interests of, among other things, morality, sovereignty and integrity of the state, public order and friendly relations with foreign states. It is this limiting clause that is often used to justify restraints on speech. But these restraints should be by way of laws made by the state, not judicial decrees, in order for them to be enforceable.

"Judicial orders are not 'law'," Gautam

They weren't sure that a failure to stand up for the anthem was a crime

Bhatia, a lawyer and author of a seminal book on free speech in India, told Index. "Freedom of speech can only be restricted by law made by the state." The Supreme Court's order, Bhatia added, exemplified a trend, →

→ where the court encourages pleas from motley groups of petitioners aimed at securing directions to enforce patriotism. "Instead of dismissing the petition on the ground that this is parliament's job, the court hears it and decides to censor speech of its own accord," Bhatia said.

Threats to free speech in India are nothing new. But judicially-enforced censorship, in a debate that is increasingly framed in nationalistic terms, appears to be a recent development.

"It is an outcome of the nationalistic politics pursued by the government," journalist Salil Tripathi told Index. "The Supreme Court order gives the emotion a sanctity." Recently a lecture by India's finance minister Arun Jaitley suggested "reasonable" restric-

The message is very clear: no dissenting voices of any consequence will be allowed

tions on free speech in the national interest should be allowed.

This trend is one that Manohar and David believe must be fought. In their conversations with Index, they were clear that they respected the national anthem; indeed, they felt pride in singing it. But the court forcing them to stand up for it struck at the core of their foundational liberties.

"My decision not to stand is part of a principled position," Manohar said. "I am completely opposed to the ruling. It's not that I don't otherwise stand up for the anthem, but to tell us that we must stand up for it to show our respect for it is simply wrong. The court can't force-feed patriotism. What's also worrying is that the order comes at a time when the ruling BJP government is already taking many steps to curb our free speech."

Manohar was hinting at the government's

wider efforts to suppress civil society movements. One of these moves has involved the cancellation of licences to about 10,000 non-governmental groups, under the Foreign Contributions Regulation Act. The law makes it mandatory for non-governmental organisations that seek foreign donations to register themselves, and it bans the use of such funds for "activities detrimental to the national interest".

"The large-scale cancellation of licences is only cover to target specific organisations which do not share the present regime's world view," Alok Prassana Kumar, a lawyer and policy expert, told Index. "The message is very clear: no dissenting voices of any consequence will be allowed."

While the order mandating respect for the national anthem can seem trivial in comparison with the government's decision to cancel licences of NGOs that act against apparent "national interest", the actions share a common thread in that they seek to enforce the state's own vision of nationalism. In the novelist Nilanjana Roy's words, we are at an important juncture in India's democracy, where there exists a serious clash of values between the rights that the constitution provides and the notions of patriotism that the state is seeking to enforce by fiat.

"There comes a time in most democracies where we start to debate the idea of freedom itself," Roy told Index. "We have a tradition of questioning in India. We need to garner this in a meaningful way."

Roy warns that if there is not a stronger movement against state-sanctioned censorship, India "could very quickly have a Turkey-like situation. Or we could even go down the path taken by other south Asian democracies, where disciplined nationalism, even at the cost of liberty, is seen as a virtue." ⊗

Suhrith Parthasarathy is a writer and lawyer, who regularly contributes to Index on Censorship magazine. He lives in Chennai, India

Poland: Special Focus

In just a few years Poland has slid from free
expression rising star to attacks on the media.
Two leading commentators analyse why

PICTURED: Govern-
ing Law and Justice
party (PiS) parlia-
mentarians during
a controversial ses-
sion of parliament
on 16 December
2016

Divide to rule

POLAND: SPECIAL FOCUS

46(01): 70/73 I DOI: 10.1177/0306422017703617

Magazine editor **Wojciech Przybylski** discusses the government's attempt to stifle news in Poland and what journalists can do to fight back

WATCHING DONALD TRUMP'S press spokesperson, Sean Spicer, give his first media briefings reminded me of how, just a year ago, the government in Poland began its illiberal revolution.

To a political commentator and editor like me, who has worked in journalism for 14 years, there are challenges on all levels. In the editorial teams of Res Publica and Visegrad Insight, journals about culture and politics, we face all sorts of dilemmas.

The first and most important dilemma arose shortly after the ruling Law and Justice Party (PiS) government effectively took over control of public service media by giving themselves powers to appoint the heads of state broadcasters.

Our quandary was then whether we should accept invitations to appear on public radio and TV programmes where our presence as independent commentators might suggest that government-controlled outlets were impartial. Or whether not to appear, which would mean we ignored part of the public which is still their audience. We decided to take part in public debates and trained ourselves to keep focused on the issues we mostly deal with, while avoiding partisan debates.

Lack of transparency and limited access to information does not help produce better quality journalism. On the contrary, in the mediocre media world we inhabit, it is hard to imagine that there will be less reporting or less news. Media outlets compete for attention and will continue to produce articles, even if their sources become less credible.

There will be more secret recordings, leaks

CREDIT: Sławomir Kamiński/Reuters

and gossip, instead of fact-checked news. Verifying facts will become an even greater challenge. We are therefore trying to build up our data by relying on in-house research, instead of more interaction with public administrators. This has its limits. At the end of the day we still ask politicians and public officials for comment, while expecting them to be less responsive.

In fact, the Polish government is officially reducing our access to politicians and public officials. On 15 December 2016 the chancellery of the Sejm, the lower house of the Polish parliament, introduced new regulations allowing only two media correspondents per outlet to observe and report on parliamentary proceedings.

In response media across all non-governmental platforms organised a protest and on 17 December journalists' accreditations were suspended for an indefinite period and they were not admitted to the building for the final proceedings of the budget session.

The protest quickly turned into a →

ABOVE: Journalists wait outside a closed door at parliament's press gallery in Warsaw, January 2017

CASES IN POINT

• Maciej Kluczka, a journalist at Poznan's branch of the government-controlled station Radio Merkury, was dismissed as host of the morning talk-show Kluczowy Temat after a critical interview with MP Ryszard Czarnecki
• The new chair of the Polish constitutional court, Julia Przyłębska, announced a ban on all photography, sound and film recordings from hearings in the court's smaller hall
• The ruling party of the Polish government blocked journalists from recording a vote on next year's budget, by organising it outside the main chamber of parliament
Source: mappingmediafreedom.org

→ political spectacle, and became a struggle between the opposition, which was arguing for the media to have access to parliamentary proceedings, and the government. Opposition politicians protested by recording selected events, but their antics and portrayal

They are freezing out established media outlets that have not been adhering to PiS's point of view

of themselves as victims meant the case for a free media took a back seat.

The outcome of the protests remains unclear. On the one hand the media ban on reporting parliamentary proceedings has been lifted, but further sanctions on media freedom are expected.

Another major challenge for Polish journalism comes from the business side. Like in other countries, it is becoming increasingly difficult to financially sustain many media outlets. Today direct sales, subscriptions and donations from readers provide only about 15% of income for magazines like ours. Public grants provide some 30%, and the rest come from a variety of private sources such as media partnerships.

The system of public subsidies that used to support independent cultural journalism is even less transparent than it was. And there are new ideological criteria on the horizon, which demand that culture which is subsidised promotes a certain kind of Polish nationalism. So, it worries us that we may end up relying on private money alone. We are concerned that our attempts to report and promote culture as we see fit will be underfunded.

Sustainability could lie with foreign donors, but we worry that access to such funding will also soon be under threat as it has been in Hungary. There, new governmental policies are attempting to curtail the activities of foreign-backed civil society groups. Already reports from March 2017 quote Barbara Bublin from PiS as saying efforts will be taken to remove foreign influence from media.

And in Poland, as in Hungary, public subsidies are made available nearly exclusively to new private media owned by businessmen with direct links to the ruling party. Public broadcasting is being taken over by the government, and attempts to gain freedom of information are being hampered by new legal restrictions.

The government is promoting start-up "news" outlets such as Gazeta Polska Codziennie daily and TV Republika that were actively supportive in the election campaign.

At the same time, they are freezing out established media outlets that have not been adhering to PiS's point of view such as Gazeta Wyborcza daily, Newsweek Polska weekly and TVN channel.

Our government has also stopped publicly financed institutions, such as ministries, agencies, courts and diplomatic missions, subscribing to press titles that would, in the past, have been considered mainstream, while decreeing they take out new subscription orders with pro-government media.

It is true to say that the previous government favoured the mainstream media by subsidising outlets with lucrative advertisements for public companies or government-sponsored public policy information campaigns. But what we are seeing now is some titles actually banned from public institutions.

With approximately 240,000 civil servants employed by national government (and similar numbers in local government) this makes a lot of difference to a daily or weekly press where circulation is at best 180,000 in the case of Newsweek Polska, or 200,000 for Gazeta Wyborcza.

By way of justification, Deputy Minister of Justice Patryk Jaki said in early January 2016 that some titles have always had a privileged position and now the government will make sure that there will be a change in the order of privileges.

The same month the government assigned Jacek Kurski, a politician, former MP and at that time the deputy minister of culture (as well as the brother of the deputy editor of Gazeta Wyborcza) to be head of public TV. People in Poland watch on average 4.23 hours of television per day, the highest in Europe, so maintaining its autonomy is crucial.

Along with public TV, public radio statutes have been changed to enable the takeover by government supporters of executive boards, in direct violation of the role of the bi-partisan committee that previously supervised the quality of public broadcasting.

Many journalists who are not supportive of the government have been fired and the remaining ones are under threat of being fired.

Neither public outrage, nor a decline in Poland's place on media freedom indexes – Poland tumbled 29 places down the Reporters without Borders World Press Freedom

Index this year – has halted the long march through the institutions by the government.

Moreover, the government is planning to introduce new taxes to support its own TV and radio: the number of viewers, along with economic performance, has been drastically falling over the last year. To this end it will most probably try to introduce new forms of privileged access for the media it favours, and hamper the freedom of information

There will be more secret recordings, leaks and gossip, instead of fact-checked news

rights and the business of media independent from government.

Effectively, that could produce a more partisan media. It may very well be a calculation and part of the political communication strategy of powerful ex-prime minister and chair of PiS Jarosław Kaczyński, who, like many others, profits from polarisation.

A chance this strategy could fail may lie in some outlets keeping up good unbiased reporting. A promising sign of public reaction to such a strategy comes from recent reports about the independent weekly Tygodnik Powszechny, which noted a 16% increase in circulation. Its editor believes this was a result of demand for good impartial journalism. Even though the numbers are not significantly changing the odds on the market, it may be one of few ways public opinion will retain access to good quality journalism.

One can only hope that this is part of a wider public response against these attempts to manipulate their news and knowledge. ⊗

Wojciech Przybylski is editor-in-chief of Visegrad Insight, a magazine about central Europe, and chairman of the Res Publica foundation in Warsaw. He is former editor-in-chief of Eurozine, a network of European cultural journals

The past is not a foreign country

POLAND: SPECIAL FOCUS

46(01): 74/76 | DOI: 10.1177/0306422017703934

As a new Polish history museum opens in Gdansk, a jigsaw of censorship and counter stories are rewriting the country's story of itself. Historian **Marcin Król** examines the past for insight into today's battles

IN 1827, A Polish censor who worked for the Russians commended censorship on the basis of there being no need for common people to know too much. That seems relevant today as the populist government makes a determined attempt to shrink public knowledge.

After the fall of the Soviet bloc, Poland shot up the ratings in the indexes for freedom of expression and enjoyed a period of international acclaim. But when the Law and Justice party (PiS) won the elections in 2015, censorship returned almost immediately as the new government took aim at neutral institutions and news outlets.

After 1945, a small handful of people formed an underground resistance movement against Soviet occupation. Now the government is trying to overstate their role to create an impression that many Poles resisted the Communists. Through this and many similar examples a new historic narrative is being created. Real facts are being replaced by a patriotic fairy tale.

The danger now is that many people are not in a position to fact-check information. They are prone to trust it. Fact-checking is made even harder as the state has always had de facto control over public television and public radio. And while there is competition from privately owned and independent television networks and newspapers, such as the Gazeta Wyborcza, a large number of people still watch and are influenced by public television, as well as listening to public radio.

In a recent case, a journalist who worked for the state-owned national television company announced in a report that a leader of one of the biggest opposition parties had been accused of spying for the Russians and arrested. The reporter mentioned his first name, so everybody knew about whom he was speaking. After an hour he backtracked on the story saying he was talking about "alternative facts".

This is important, because the current government's intention also includes disseminating a false story about Poland past and present. Because of that officials can say that freedom of speech is maintained, but challenge reports that do not agree with their version of events.

Following World War II, censorship under the Communists was omnipresent. State media was a channel for the ruling party. All media outlets were controlled, even the very few that were, from the point of view of ownership, independent, and mainly Catholic. In response, writers got savvy. A characteristic

Real facts are being replaced by a patriotic fairy tale

interplay developed between authors and their readership, with the media using hints and allusions to let their audience know what the real story was. These became well known and could be immediately picked up.

A period of much greater media freedom between 1990 and 2015 was internationally acknowledged. In a report by the Pew Research Centre, which compiled data in 2015, Poland secured second place in the ranking measuring freedom of speech and expression, just behind the USA and ahead of Germany, France and the UK. Censorship never completely went away though. During this period, laws on offending religious feelings were used at times against critical artistic works. Artist Dorota Nieznalska fell foul of these laws in 2003 when she was sentenced by a court to six months' imprisonment for her piece entitled Passion, depicting male genitals in the shape of a cross. Her trial lasted seven years until she was eventually acquitted.

Given the historical backdrop, it was hardly surprising that, when PiS won the elections in 2015, censorship returned almost immediately. This type of censorship is reminiscent of absolute monarchs or the notion put forward in George Orwell's novel, 1984. Within a few months of their accession to power, PiS had passed an amendment to Poland's media →

OPPOSITE: Graffiti demanding freedom of expression for Polish press, radio and TV in 1981

→ law. It removed senior figures who managed the country's public television and radio broadcasters, and gave power to the treasury minister to hire their successors. Writing an opinion piece for Radio Maryja, Krystyna Pawlowicz, an outspoken PiS member of parliament said that the idea of an apolitical media is a "harmful idealised myth" which makes it harder to govern.

Censorship aimed at re-creating a new story of the Polish past, its symbols and myths, is also evident in the case of Smoleńsk, the 2010 plane crash, in which the then-President Leck Kaczyński died. He was the twin brother of the ex-prime minister and powerful current chairman of PiS, Jarosław Kaczynski. The crash was declared an accident at the time. Now Kaczyński and others are presenting it as an assassination, with speculation cast on the Russians or the Polish

Hundreds of people have been dismissed from their positions at public television and radio

leadership, in particular that of Donald Tusk, who was prime minister of Poland at the time of the crash. Meanwhile in Gdansk the new Museum of the Second World War is seen to be under pressure to present a story of Polish history that the government prefers.

I was offered the job of head of the broadcasting authority in 1989. However, the then prime minister, Tadeusz Mazowiecki, demanded that the position be subordinate to government interests, which resulted in my rejection of the job.

Now things have gone much further. Hundreds of people have been dismissed from their positions at public television and radio broadcasters. This did not just include those who were actively against the ruling party, it also included those who hadn't take a stance. But while this has resulted in a drastic fall in the

standards of public television, only parts of the viewership are aware of it.

Current censorship stretches far beyond the media. Through being a member of various monitoring bodies, the government exerts huge influence on cultural politics. This is the case with theatres, some of the biggest of which are state-owned and state subsidised. Even Polish cultural institutions abroad are subject to censorship. The government is recommending right-wing writers from the second ranks and forgetting about great authors who hold different views. This results in an absurd situation in which works are promoted that no one is interested in.

Privately owned businesses are not free from the state's grasp either, and this might be the most dangerous censorship of all as it is the most opaque. Private television and magazines face a precarious future, with advertising being hard to come by. At present, large to medium-sized private TV channels are largely unaffected, but it's been disastrous for dailies and weeklies, where the situation is already precarious because of the crisis within print journalism.

The only beacon of hope right now is the internet, which is, as yet, uncensored.

Censorship in Poland threatens not only our access to information, but also our politics. While the opposition is busy pointing out the lies told by ruling authorities, there is a risk that it will eventually stop thinking long term. It could result in the erosion of fact, as well as the erosion of control. We are at risk of sinking into a world of lies from which it will be very hard to escape. Such unreality arises as a result of manifold censorship acts everywhere, in public life and, gradually, in the private realm. ⊗

*Translated by **Martha Otwinowski***

***Marcin Król** is a historian of ideas at the University of Warsaw and a former magazine editor and columnist. He is also a winner of the literary Kościelski Award*

Shooting from the hip

46(01): 77/79 I DOI: 10.1177/0306422017703618

Former TV anchor Armando Cabada Alvídrez has recently taken over as mayor of Mexican border town Ciudad Juárez. **Irene Caselli** asks him what he can do to address violent attacks on the media

LYING ON THE US border, where President Donald Trump is promising a new wall, the state of Chihuahua has a frightening record for journalist security. At the end of 2016, radio reporter Jesús Adrián Rodríguez Samaniego was shot dead outside his home. Then Miroslava Breach Velducea, who worked for one of Mexico's best-known newspapers La Journada, was murdered in March 2017.

But earlier this year when Index on Censorship interviewed Armando Cabada Alvídrez, the mayor of the largest city in Chihuahua, he was feeling positive about journalist safety. "We have no information that alarms us now. Just imagine, I come from that profession. If I had any information that suggested that there is a risk for journalists, I would summon them and warn them. I would look after them," he said at his office in Ciudad Juárez.

Prior to becoming mayor in October, Cabada was the best known TV anchor in the city and now argues the situation has improved.

Cabada added: "There is a closeness to journalists here. If journalists were to provide any information that suggested a risk for them, we would deal with it immediately.

My colleagues in the media have understood very well the message of criminal groups. If you do your work professionally, if you don't get involved with them, there is no reason to be in danger."

Pressed on the question of danger, he added: "I can tell you that more than 90% of the homicides that have taken place since we took over have to do with those who dedicate themselves to this criminal business. This is why Juárez is a city that is safe for its visitors, despite the alert issued by the US State Department. It is safe for its own residents too, for good people, for those who do not dedicate themselves to that business, which is the great majority."

Mexico was ranked 149th out of 180 countries in the Reporters without Borders' 2016 World Press Freedom Index. It's a country where media can be influenced by government money and attacks against journalists are common, but rarely investigated. The mayor argued that other areas in Mexico are worse for journalists. "In areas of the south or in Nuevo Laredo, for example, it is forbidden as a journalist to handle information about drug trafficking, because it can cost your life. Here, this is not the case. Luckily in Juárez this does not happen." →

OPPOSITE: Former TV anchor Armando Cabada Alvídrez at his new mayoral office in Ciudad Juárez. Several journalists have been murdered in recent years in the city

→ But journalists are sceptical of the new mayor's ability to make a difference. "The majority of attacks we receive come from the security forces, not from organised crime," said Gabriela Minjares, one of the co-founders of the Juárez Journalists' Network. In 2011, Minjares created the network, together with other female reporters, after two colleagues were killed. "There is a complicity: the police forces are permeated by organised crime. They have not been cleaned up."

Index asked the mayor specifically about the role of the security forces in threatening journalists. He replied by saying that the times have changed.

"It is clear to me what kind of authorities we had at the time. They were policemen that literally worked for the delinquents, they were at the payroll of the criminals. Luckily, there was a purge."

In 2007, drug cartels started fighting over local territory, because of the city's strategic value on the smuggling routes from South America to the USA. At the height of the violence, in 2010, an average of 10 people were murdered every day. Kidnappings, carjacking and extortion also soared. Journalists were among the victims: four reporters

If I had any information that suggested that there is a risk for journalists, I would summon them and warn them

were killed in Ciudad Juárez between 2008 and 2012, and many were intimidated and threatened. The Mexican government eventually deployed soldiers in armoured vehicles to patrol the city's streets.

Cabada pointed out that he had personal experience of working as a journalist and being under pressure. In 2008 he started receiving death threats via email, which led to his flight across the border to El Paso, Texas.

"I was threatened because we did not change our editorial line," claimed Cabada. TV station Canal 44 belonged to his family and became well known for its daily coverage of murders. It developed a system of mobile units that often reached murder scenes as quickly as the police.

"I had to take precautionary measures. I had to find an armoured vehicle for every time I crossed back into Ciudad Juárez. I had to take my family with me to the USA. We lost our freedom to live how we used to," he said.

Cabada lived in El Paso for four years. During that time, he continued anchoring an evening newscast from a US studio. In January last year, Cabada announced he would run for mayor on an independent platform.

During his electoral campaign, "narcomantas" (usually large white bedsheets with painted messages, common in Mexico's drug war) appeared, linking Cabada to a cartel. Cabada denied any links, though he said his wife was previously married to someone with links, albeit ones she was unaware of at the time. These accusations did not affect his campaign. He went on to earn 49% of the vote.

"My main commitment is to provide tranquility to all Juarenses [people from Ciudad Juárez]. It is my obligation as a mayor. It is not just for one particular group," Cabada told Index.

He said he would keep up the fight against corruption within the police force, foster transparency and bring down murder rates. As for the US border, he was feeling positive about that too.

"We have an excellent relationship with US authorities on the other side of the border and collaborate with El Paso on border patrol issues. We have always had a life in common. We don't have to worry."

But Minjares doesn't have much faith in Cabada, and she sees colleagues giving up on journalism. "Every time I hear that a colleague is leaving the profession, I feel

sadness. It is a clear sign of how much our work conditions have deteriorated."

"Cabada always stayed on his set. He left for El Paso when violence flared up. There is a big difference between us reporters, the troop who always worked here, and him. I don't consider him a journalist," she said.

Cabada is now six months into his two years in office. He looks back at his days as an anchor with nostalgia. "It is easier to ask questions than to be questioned," he said.

Whether that is the case is debatable. History paints a different picture when it comes to being a journalist in Ciudad Juárez. As for whether it can be the case moving forward, that will be partly up to Cabada. ⊗

Irene Caselli is a freelance journalist based in Argentina and a contributing editor for Index on Censorship magazine. She was a 2016 Adelante Latin America Reporting Fellow with the International Women's Media Foundation

Silence in the House

46(01): 80/81 I DOI: 10.1177/0306422017703620

Discussions of difficult subjects are not taking place in the UK's parliament, says former attorney general **Dominic Grieve**

EVERY GENERATION DEVELOPS its own taboos, subjects that simply do not get discussed because they are deemed too controversial or offensive to public order. Those people who do attempt to talk about them can find themselves both criticised and ostracised.

At present, we can see this in the rise of political correctness at universities, with "no platform" policies towards anyone raising any of a range of topics. "Safe space" has become a place not for rational and moderate debate on sensitive subjects but for closing it down altogether. According to the most recent annual survey of UK universities by online magazine Spiked, just under two thirds of student unions have actively censored the free expression of ideas on campus, including on wholly lawful viewpoints such as opposing abortion. Even more worryingly, nearly a quarter of university administrations have joined in this process of banning lawful comment on subjects which they consider might offend the principles of political correctness that they have embraced.

But this trend is not confined to places of learning. At a national political level, it is becoming harder to articulate views that depart from current norms. It is ironic that as we strive to develop a pluralist and tolerant multicultural society, we end up imposing new orthodoxies as substitutes for the old. Thus those who espouse Christian beliefs and ethics, whilst being perfectly tolerant of those who disagree with them, find themselves "tolerated" but sometimes unable to promote publicly their point of view.

A few years ago, I had a constituent who was a street preacher threatened with prosecution under the Public Order Act for saying that if people did not repent and turn to God they were at risk of going to hell. The police told him that the mention of the "risk of going to hell" was abusive and threatening! Fortunately, wiser counsel prevailed and the case was dropped. But it illustrated the risk of how laws thoughtlessly applied can have a chilling effect on expressions of deeply held personal opinion that the individual concerned clearly thought was important to communicate to others.

Twenty years in parliament has also taught me that attempts at avoiding difficult subjects, for the sake of mitigating controversy or giving offence, are often counterproductive. One of the problems with modern politics is that it has become increasingly presentational, so that the messaging becomes an end in itself and a form of advertising that seeks to ingratiate itself with its audience and avoid confrontation. As a result, the proper discussion of difficult subjects never takes place because such debates are not seen as the generator of short-term electoral support. This has happened consistently, for example, over immigration, where mainstream politicians have refused to engage with the public over their concerns.

CREDIT: UK Parliament/Mark Duffy

As a result, the issue has been allowed to develop without a reasoned examination of the underlying drivers. The consequence could be clearly seen in the way immigration became a matter of great importance during the EU referendum campaign and by the manner in which the Remain campaign was incapable of responding to the issue.

Yet one of the best features of our human condition should be our ability to communicate and exchange ideas. It is what has taken us in 10,000 years from living in caves to our present state of advancement. This has been underpinned by our ability to moderate each other's views by open debate, and it is those societies where this has happened the most which have been at the forefront of this process. The extraordinary explosion of information exchange now possible through the internet is accelerating this exponentially. It highlights the counterproductiveness of trying to restrict or censor the free exchange of information and opinion. Yet even today in Britain there are attempts at doing this, often by those who claim to support freedom of expression.

This is not to say that there should be a free-for-all. There are sound reasons for many of our existing laws in this area. We must, of necessity, maintain laws on contempt of court to allow jury trials to proceed without hindrance and ensure fairness in court proceedings. I have no difficulty with libel laws that allow a person to get redress through the courts for serious damage to their reputation. And laws against the incitement to violence or irrational hatred on the basis of race, gender or sexual orientation are plainly needed.

But we should always be very wary of any extensions on restrictions to freedom of speech. Recent suggestions that expressions of non-violent extremism should be criminalised are likely to encourage the development of extreme views rather than reduce their occurrence. A robust willingness to challenge views with which one profoundly

disagrees is much more likely to succeed in the long term.

So there is a great need today for those who see freedom of expression as a key to successful human societies to speak out for what we believe in. It has been one of my greatest pleasures as an MP that when we successfully challenged the original draft of the legislation on incitement to religious hatred so as to remove "insulting words" from the text, it brought together human-

ABOVE: UK Prime Minister Theresa May at the dispatch box in parliament

Twenty years in parliament has also taught me that attempts at avoiding difficult subjects, for the sake of mitigating controversy or giving offence, are often counterproductive

ists, people of different faiths, and writers and comics in an alliance. We will doubtless need more of this co-operation, as well as common sense, as we continue to face challenges in this area in the future. ⊗

Dominic Grieve is an MP in the UK parliament and a former attorney general

Puppet masters

46(01): 82/84 I DOI: 10.1177/0306422017703621

Roger Law, one of the creators of the UK's most influential TV satire show Spitting Image, talks Trump and what satirists need to do now

SPITTING IMAGE OWED a great deal to the great British caricaturist James Gillray, possibly even a royalty payment. Gillray's powerful images of the crimes and misdemeanors of the great and the good in the late 18th and early 19th century are recycled by each generation of cartoonists. The fact that the great man gets updated by talents such as Gerald Scarfe, Peter Brookes, Steve Bell and many others testifies to this. I am told on good authority that when we Brits were cosying up to the Spanish during the Napoleonic Wars, Gillray's prints became popular in Spain, and the painter Francisco Goya came into possession of some. Whilst I hesitate to say that Goya lifted them, he certainly made a few etchings that paid "homage" to Gillray. Spitting Image, I'm afraid, had no shame in reworking the master.

To deliver satirical jibes effectively, it helps to be around at the right time. Spitting Image set up shop when the country was deeply divided. Riots on the streets were the order of the day – the police versus the miners, protests against the poll tax and more. Feelings were running very high. Personally I would have killed my mother to make Spitting Image. I was angry and I really wanted to do that kind of television satire. Spitting Image had British Prime Minister Margaret Thatcher and US President Ronald Reagan and a robust couple of decades obsessed with war, money and celebrity. Gillray had

British Prime Minister William Pitt and French Emperor Napoleon Bonaparte and a robust couple of decades also obsessed with war, money and celebrity.

Peter Fluck, my partner in crime, and I had been making caricatures for print for 20 years before we struck out with the satirical puppet show Spitting Image. With hindsight, possibly our only achievement was to take political cartooning from print to television. Although it was not easy to convince television programme controllers to back the idea, the time was right. Charles Denton of Central Television decided to sprinkle the holy water on the project and backed us to the hilt.

Good satire comes out of conflict. In the present climate of division, fueled by Brexit in the UK and President Donald Trump in the White House, the long established British satirical magazine, Private Eye, is enjoying the highest circulation in the publication's history. (Ian Hislop, the current editor of Private Eye, cut his teeth writing for the first series of Spitting Image.) NBC's Saturday Night Live has been running in the USA for as long as I can remember. With the dissent Trump is causing, their ratings are up by 60% from a year ago.

Although an extremely cumbersome way to make television, the Spitting Image puppets had a huge advantage over actors. Viewers will accept the rudeness, violence and

CREDIT: Spitting Image Workshop

disorder on screen because the protagonists are puppets. Mr Punch of Punch and Judy is an alcoholic wife beater and serial murderer who repeatedly whacks his baby for crying, yet young children adore him. Spitting Image puppets likewise moved from one sketch to another with mayhem and violence accepted by 15 million viewers on a Sunday evening. It is hard for actors to be relentlessly rude and unpleasant whilst nurturing a career, and perhaps playing tennis with their victims. Puppets have no agents or careers and, after the show, can be hung up in a cupboard.

The long tradition of satire in England might explain why caricature and satire is tolerated. Spitting Image on television astonishingly had less censorship than Fluck and I had experienced when working for print. Years of editorial control had conditioned us to what it was possible to get away with when working for publications such as The Sunday Times, The New York Times and European magazines. But our workshop rule was not to censor ourselves as there were plenty of people who would do just that.

We put out some raunchy royal →

ABOVE: Then Prime Minister Margaret Thatcher lampooned in the Spitting Image television show

→ sketches on Spitting Image. But it was the image published in The Appallingly Disrespectful Spitting Image Book of the young Duke of York (Prince Andrew) reclining nude in silk sheets with two pounds of Cumberland sausages nestling between his hairy thighs that caused the royals to reach for the Director of Public Prosecutions. "This time they have gone too far!" To which a wise DPP advised: "Don't do it Ma'am. These people will turn up in court with the effigy and the sausages." And we would have done.

I still find the difference in freedom between print and television puzzling. My theory is that the English only take gardening and literature seriously. Television is visual and ephemeral; after all, "It's only TV."

Does satire change anything? Not really from my experience. However whilst Spitting Image was on air its audience knew

ITV seem not to have the vision or budgets for another Spitting Image

what was going on and who the perpetrators were. Unfortunately it cut both ways. Spitting Image became such essential viewing for members of parliament that on Monday morning Central Television would deliver a video tape to Westminster for those who had missed the show the night before.

Good satire, like a good joke, can be a superior way to tell the truth. Max Beerbohm, the dapper British Edwardian caricaturist, said he could never look at a hot water bottle without thinking of King Henry VIII.

Consequently, neither can I. And Francis Bacon said that "a good portrait has to do some damage", which I think our caricatures did. Such is the power of visual satire that Spitting Image did change the viewer's perception of public figures. For example the slug-like Education Secretary Kenneth Baker or the leader of the Social Democratic Party David Owen with the whining, bed-wetting

Liberal leader David Steel in his pocket. This visual subversion even played tricks with me.

After Thatcher's election triumph in 1987 I asked my wife if she'd seen photographs of the new cabinet on the front page of The Sunday Times. "Those are your Spitting Image puppets, you dope, not photos of the real people!" she said. I began to realise, with delight, that other people had acquired the same ability to confuse the puppet and their behaviour with that of the person; no mean feat considering the great lengths and amount of money the powerful in public life spend on public relations. David Cameron (the most ineffectual prime minister in decades) was in public relations before he came to power and "it will never happen again" became his mantra.

If only for this reason I think satire is important. At the time of writing President Trump is trying to bypass the news media with relentless insults and censorship, using his tweets and rallies to publicise the "truth" as he sees it with the cry "the enemy of the people" levelled at the BBC, CNN and The New York Times.

Satire is only able to lance the boil from time to time. But it is worth doing. ITV seem not to have the vision or budgets for another Spitting Image and I doubt very much that the BBC, with their remit for balance, would ever commission such a show. The dark side of the Scottish comedian Frankie Boyle is getting a hearing, but are there any angry young satirists out there to help him? The rise of nationalism in Europe and the boil that is President Trump are in urgent need of lancing. The grave danger is that censorship and alternative truths will win out as they did before, in the 1930s. ⊗

Roger Law is the co-creator of the 1980s TV series Spitting Image

Drawing the line

46(01): 85/87 | DOI: 10.1177/0306422017703622

Cartoonist Bill Leak felt Australia's Racial Discrimination Act was limiting free speech. **John Power** asked Leak why in one of the last interviews before Leak's death

HE WAS ONE of Australia's most irreverent cartoonists. In the months leading up to his death in March 2017, Bill Leak had been one of the loudest voices in a simmering debate on how to balance freedom of expression and the protection of racial minorities.

Both on and off the page, the cartoonist with The Australian newspaper had positioned himself as a leading critic of a contested clause of the 1975 Racial Discrimination Act, Section 18C, which makes it unlawful to "offend, insult, humiliate or intimidate" a person because of their race or ethnicity.

Opposition to the law, primarily from the political right, has grown ever since 2011, when one of Australia's most prominent conservative commentators, Andrew Bolt, was found to have contravened the act. The federal court ruled Bolt had breached Section 18C in a series of columns where he implied that a group of light-skinned aboriginals had played up their heritage for personal gain.

The debate is now firmly on the public agenda following several high profile and contentious cases involving Section 18C last year. Under the current government, pressure

from MPs led to Prime Minister Malcolm Turnbull going ahead with a parliamentary inquiry into amending Section 18C. A report issued in February as part of the inquiry said no changes were necessary. But Turnbull is suggesting he will take action.

"We've got people emerging who, when you talk to them about freedom of speech, they think that it's the legal right to abuse people on the bus," Leak told Index on Censorship magazine, describing what he believed was a dangerous and prevalent ignorance enshrined in the legal code. "They don't actually understand that it's thanks →

ABOVE: Cartoonist Bill Leak, whose work had seen him being threatened with court and forced to move house

→ to freedom of speech that we live in a free democracy."

One of the most controversial recent cases, which sparked the inquiry, involved a lawsuit brought under Section 18C against three university students who complained about being denied entry into a computer room reserved for indigenous students. The lawsuit was thrown out by the federal court.

But the case that most animated Leak involved the cartoonist himself. His critique of parental neglect in remote aboriginal communities put him in Section 18C's crosshairs when it was published last August.

The cartoon depicts a policeman telling a seemingly drunk aboriginal man to talk to his son about responsibility. The father replies that he does not remember the boy's name. The cartoon became the subject of an investigation by the Australian Human Rights Commission after several members of the public lodged complaints.

In Leak's case, the main complainant withdrew, saying the cartoonist did not have interest in AHRC-facilitated conciliation and his newspaper The Australian wanted the case to go to court. She said she would have a slim hope of success in court because of exceptions in the law for expression, made "reasonably and in good faith", which is artistic or in the public interest.

Usually, the AHRC negotiates a solution between parties, which can include a monetary settlement or formal apology. But if mediation fails, the matter goes to court. Leak and other critics of Section 18C argued that even if vindicated in court, the process was its own punishment. Beyond a significant emotional toll, the legal fees could be exorbitant.

"It has been used as an instrument with which to punish someone, like me, for having defied the unwritten rules of political correctness," said Leak.

"What frightens me about this is it reeks of authoritarianism."

In a 2017 report Amnesty International defends Section 18C and argues that the courts have struck "the balance well by protecting our freedom of expression as well as protecting people from racial hatred."

Many ethnic and religious lobby groups, such as the Ethnic Communities Council of Victoria and the Executive Council of Australian Jewry, are opposed to changing the law, as are MPs from the Labour Party and Australian Greens, the main opposition parties. Then there are those opposing changes in the media, including prominent journalist Richard Ackland, who has questioned what it is critics of the law want to say so badly.

But the Media, Entertainment & Arts Alliance, the main union representing journalists, has taken a more middle-of-the-road stance. In its submission to the parliamentary inquiry, the union suggested replacing the terms "insult" and "offend" with "vilify".

Leak was born in Adelaide in 1956 and has had his work published in Australian newspapers for decades. His recent cartoon was not the first time he'd come under fire.

In 2015, he had to move house after authorities warned him that his ode to the slain staff at Charlie Hebdo featuring Jesus and Mohammed made him a target of Islamists.

"Everything is open to criticism, everything is open to ridicule, your silly fucking prophet included," Leak said. "Jesus Christ cops a hell of a hiding and everyone just laughs. And I just thought, well it would be wonderful if everyone just sort of does a cartoon, Mohammed's in it, and then it becomes a non-issue."

Leak thought he'd be joined by his fellow cartoonists in defending free expression, but instead he said he encountered an attitude of "Leak brought that on himself".

"When it comes to expressing themselves, they haven't even paused and thought: 'Wait a minute, without the freedom to express my own ideas and to say what I want to say, I haven't got a job,'" said Leak. Robert Russell of Cartoonists Rights Network International told Index: "Cartoonists are the canary in

SECTION 18C TIMELINE

1975: Racial Discrimination Act passes, outlawing unfair treatment based on "race, colour, or national or ethnic origin" in areas such as employment, education, access to public services and accommodation.

1995: Racial Hatred Act expands coverage of the RDA to include "hate speech" and "racial vilification". Section 18C states that a public act is unlawful if it is motivated by ethnicity and is "reasonably likely, in all the circumstances, to offend, insult, humiliate or intimidate another person or a group of people".

2009: Journalist Andrew Bolt writes in the Herald Sun accusing several light-skinned aboriginal people of claiming to be aboriginal for personal gain. He was sued under the RDA. Bolt argued that this was his honestly held opinion on a matter of public interest, but in 2011 a judge ruled that Bolt's comments were "inflammatory, provocative and cynical". This case is regarded as the catalyst for calls to reform Section 18C.

2014: Prime Minister Tony Abbott proposes reforms to the phrasing of Section 18C, taking issue with interpretation of "offend" and "insult", but then backs down.

2016: Bill Leak's cartoon featuring an apparently drunk aboriginal man forgetting his son's name is published by The Australian. The newspaper defended the cartoon, saying Leak was addressing a "core issue". Meanwhile, senators including David Leyonhjelm and Malcolm Roberts proposed completely repealing Section 18C and "everything that goes along with it".

2017: The joint parliamentary committee on human rights makes no recommendations to change Section 18C.

---

the coal mine when it comes to free speech. They are among the first journalists to be singled out for criticism and held up as examples of free speech excesses, often by conservative elements that are disturbed by the disturbing fringes of free speech."

For years, Leak had upset sensibilities by aiming his pencil at subjects including feminism, the lesbian, gay, bisexual and transgender lobby and environmental activists.

Though drawn to left-wing politics as a young man, Leak felt that the left had moved far from ideals it once championed.

"People who regard themselves as left wing these days are censorious, they are the people who are most in favour of limiting freedom of speech," Leak said.

Leak believed that too few people understood the value of pushing the boundaries of discourse. He argued that critics who labelled him racist for his cartoon about aboriginal fathers, for instance, missed the point, and were avoiding discussion of a real problem affecting some indigenous children.

"What about their human rights? They don't count," Leak said. "The human right not to be offended is the one that counts, and there is no such thing."

While detractors would paint him as "Australia's leading racist," Leak was adamant he treated everyone as an individual regardless of race.

Leak was unconvinced Section 18C would be repealed, but he was convinced the fight should go on. ⊗

John Power is a freelance journalist based in Melbourne, Australia. He tweets @John_F_Power

Puppet state

46(01): 88/89 I DOI: 10.1177/0306422017703623

After two Spanish puppeteers were arrested for a scene from their show, **Alfonso Lázaro de la Fuente** talks about their terrible year and his fears for other artists ending up in prison

A SCENE FEATURING A policeman and a witch carrying a banner referring to the fictional terrorist organisation Alka-ETA was the part of our Punch and Judy show that sparked our arrest. The consequences led to an extraordinary year for me and my fellow puppeteer Raúl García Pérez.

After being arrested and charged, we struggled to get work. We were banned from leaving the country and became victims of a vicious media attack, all because of a puppet show.

It began with a performance of La Bruja y Don Cristóbal (The Witch and Don Cristóbal), which we staged as part of the carnival festivities in Madrid last February. Shortly after the scene with the witch, the real police arrived and arrested us. We were charged with glorifying terrorism, a crime which carries a possible jail sentence of up to four years. We were also charged with inciting hatred.

The day after our arrest we gave a statement before an investigating magistrate and, although we explained the content of the play, he sent us to prison without bail, pending trial. We remained there for five days until our lawyer was able to prove we were at no risk of flight, which had been the reason given by the prosecutor to lock us up.

But our ordeal did not end there. For the first month after our release, we could not travel abroad and had to check into our local police station daily. As a result, Raúl and I, who live in different parts of the country,

could not work together. Our lawyer appealed the decision and from 10 March Raúl had to report every 15 days and myself only once a month, because of health concerns.

Fortunately, after that we were able to tour the country and because of our raised profile, we performed to large audiences, including recently in February 2017 where we staged The Witch and Don Christóbal in Madrid. It was a sell-out performance and incident free.

It was the first time we could perform this play though as until then we were concerned we would run the risk of being arrested again. In fact, we had to continue reporting to the police right up until September 2016, when the terrorism charges were dropped.

While we found support from some members of the public, as evidenced by the success of our subsequent shows, not everyone believed our innocence, and some were outright hostile. Reporters camped outside my parents' house and called us "terrorists".

We also received anonymous threats. For example, one person wrote saying: "We know who you are and where you live and you should tread carefully." Another message attacked us and named our parents too. It said: "This is going to cost you and Adeli, Mariluz, Juanma and Carlos." These threats were later attributed to a former high-ranking member of the military.

Perhaps the most chilling aspect of our case was how easy it was to end up in our situation and what it means for other artists. We were charged with inciting hatred, which is a felony created in theory to protect vulnerable minorities. The minorities, in this case, were the church, the police and the legal system, none of which can be considered vulnerable as they wield great power. And we were charged with glorification of terrorism of a completely fictitious Alka-ETA organisation. Our lawyers compared it to charging James Bond's author with glorifying Spectre.

These are troubling times in general, especially for this form of theatre. Punch and Judy-style shows derive from the traditional Italian *commedia dell'arte*. When the church discouraged public theatre during the Reformation, travelling companies took their place and rescued one of their most iconic characters, Pulcinella (in Italian), Polichinela (in Spanish) or Mr Punch (in British popular culture). This character would mock anyone and anything seeking to oppress society. He would take on the powerful and come out winning, to the delight of the oppressed.

As in the past, Punch and Judy shows do not follow protocol. They rely on the use of sarcasm, rudeness and bad taste. The play Raúl and I put on used the same dynamics and differed only from mainstream ones in tone: it was more serious than normal. Many Punch and Judy shows tend to feature violence without any justification, but our play focused on structural violence in society. This included the injustice of private property, the church and its conservative pressure on families, and the role police forces and judges play as state oppressors. Incidentally, the intention of the scene for which we were arrested was to protest against the way police in Spain present evidence, and against the fact that many anarchists are facing terrorism charges based on flimsy evidence.

The terrorism charges were dropped in September 2016, and the hatred ones were dropped in January 2017. In the end the case never went to trial. But this only happened because in the play no character praised Alka-ETA. The sign appeared as a means of framing

the witch for a crime. It was therefore assumed we did not share the thoughts of the characters. What if one of the characters had praised terrorism? Would the court's decision have been different? Many fictitious characters commit all sorts of crimes and it troubles us that artists can be prosecuted because of what happens in their scripts. A work of fiction was judged by its content. It was assumed a playwright shared the opinions of their characters. This was an assault against creative freedom.

The consequences of two artists ending up in prison for the content of their work spreads fear among other writers. They might feel forced to revise their texts and impose limits on themselves, out of fear of being imprisoned for their work. I thought we had left behind the old Francoist mentality, which prevailed in the transition year of 1977 when members of the Catalan theatre company Els Joglars were prosecuted for performing a play, La Torna (The Return), about the trial and death sentence of two anarchists. I thought incorrectly. ⊗

*Translated by **Daniel Amelang López**, their defence lawyer*

Alfonso Lázaro de la Fuente and **Raúl García Pérez** *are professional puppeteers from Spain. They run the theatre group Títeres Desde Abajo*

ABOVE: Alfonso Lázaro de la Fuente and Raúl García Pérez with their puppets

CULTURE

IN THIS SECTION

MAIN: A woman walks past a wall with graffiti asking Egyptians to participate in
demonstrations against the Egyptian regime in Cairo, November 2016

Novel take on terror

46(01): 92/97 I DOI: 10.1177/0306422017703624

French writer and documentary maker **Karim Miské** was horrified when the Paris neighbourhood where he set his acclaimed debut novel produced the Charlie Hebdo attackers. **Sally Gimson** talks to him about his fascination with crime and introduces an original short story, translated for the first time into English

KARIM MISKÉ IS one of the most original writers to hit the French literary scene in the last five years. His debut novel Arab Jazz won the Grand Prix de Littérature Policière, France's prestigious crime writing prize. And his most recent work, half essay, half autobiography N'appartenir (Not Belonging) has just been published as a graphic novel.

The most astonishing aspect of Arab Jazz, set in Paris's multicultural 19th arrondissement, is that the world of Salafist Muslims and orthodox Jews which inspired Miské was the one that produced Chérif and Saïd Kouachi, who carried out the terror killings in the Charlie Hebdo offices after the novel was first published.

As a documentary maker interested in fundamentalism, closed worlds and identity, perhaps Miské should not have been surprised that fiction and reality became mixed. Indeed, as he admits, he had wilfully blended the two. It still spooked him that real life terrorists ended up walking the streets of

his novel. It made him decide eventually not to do as he originally intended and write a sequel to Arab Jazz, but to start on a completely different novel.

The people who were running the country [Albania] were criminals – that was the hidden secret

"Basically I'm a documentary film maker. I made documentaries for 25 years and then I decide to write fiction and again reality intrudes," he said. "I finally understood last summer it was impossible for me to keep on writing about this story because the reality was too powerful. I could not go back to this, so I had to write a new one. I think it is not going to be a crime novel... It is going to be set in the 11th arrondissement of Paris quite close to where I live and in places I used to go and it will be the story of two →

PICTURED: Author Karim Miské has been interested in totalitarian regimes since he was a child. In his short story he imagines a dark future in which several organisations group together to govern all technology

→ millennials, two young Parisian professionals. It's set in Paris post attacks, but it is not talking about terrorism. It's just about the mood of the city."

Brought up in Paris, Miské, 52, is the son of a Mauritanian diplomat and a French mother. It was his leftist mother's admiration for Enver Hoxha, the brutal Albanian dictator who died in 1985, which first aroused his interest in totalitarianism and crime.

She took him to visit Tirana when he was eight years old as part of her research for a book on the liberation of Albanian women. Miské said he was uncomfortable at what he saw and understood there was a gap between what his mother told him (and believed) and the reality. But he did not understand the full murderous horror of the dictatorship. It is, he said, the big lie and the crime at the heart of totalitarian regimes which fascinate him.

"It was the contradiction, between the people we were seeing in Paris, the activists, the leftists who were free, but were supporting this strange country where there was no freedom," he said. "I kind of felt all this. I developed a special sensibility towards crime at that time. Because they were criminals. The people who were running the country [Albania] were criminals – that was the hidden secret. It's something I understood afterwards when I read Ismail Kadare, the Albanian writer. I understood it had been a very hard political system. Ten percent of the population were in prison or in a labour camp. Religion was forbidden, and if priests baptised children they were killed."

The short story printed below is a dystopian tale of a world taken over by criminals and governed by intrusive technology. Salvation comes in the form of a woman called Vera and her secret personal project. The story was first written in 2013 for the Maison de la Radio, home of France's public service broadcaster France Radio. Miské has updated it exclusively for Index on Censorship magazine and it has been translated into English for the first time. ⊗

Sally Gimson is a freelance journalist

Paris Calling

VÉRA DJANKOVIC WAS my great aunt. There is something unsettling about saying those words here, in this identical reconstruction of her studio, with its clocks and gadgets, its carpet, coffee cups and smells. To walk into this room is to step 60 years into the past, back to those carefree days at the start of the millennium when Véra worked on RFI's legendary morning show. It's only thanks to her and her remarkable determination that any of us remember Radio France Internationale, even though France herself, like every other nation, is no longer. But I'm going off-topic, emotions, I suppose. It's impossible for me to talk about Véra dispassionately. I loved her more than anyone else in the world. She gave my life purpose. And she saved us all. Véra.

Picture her, sat there behind her vintage mixing desk, on the morning of the last ever RFI live show from Maison de la Radio. She's swigging a gin and tonic, even though it's 6am UT.

That morning everyone was drinking. How else could they numb the pain of being uprooted from a place that meant so much to them all? There was a feverish, electric atmosphere. Devastating, in fact. Her colleagues resorted to base destruction; anything for a chance to rise again from the ashes. A curious pillaging spree set in. Nothing was spared as journalists, assistants, interns and technicians made off with bits of carpet, warning signs, microphone cables. Grounded, well-brought-up people, who under normal circumstances wouldn't even swipe a box of matches from the supermarket, began ransacking their workplace, seconds after they had been cast out despite two, ten or twenty years' loyal service. Not shown the door. No, I mean cast out, in the truest sense, from the place they had called home for so long. By forcing them to leave, the powers-that-be were taking away a part of them. Hence the frenzied need to remove, to reappropriate these objects and souvenirs. Véra helped herself to a clock with red LED digits and, soothed by the balm of the alcohol, simply sat and watched the chaos unfold around her. It was a mix of excitement and disarray, driven by a primal need to commit these illegal acts together.

As she told me some 45 years later, it was at that precise moment that the vision began to form. A relentless haze of images and words swirled round her head, fueled by gin and the febrile mood in the building. The Matrix, Terminator, De Gaulle, the impermanence of things, immanence, resistance… Leaving the radio station that had been her whole life set off a stream of consciousness that was beyond her control. A mission was taking shape in her mind. Something to do with destiny or karma. Something big, unclear and inexplicable. She felt like Noah before he built his ark, just without any gods whispering in her ear. Her path was mapped out and nothing would get in her way.

Using her pass and her intricate knowledge of the premises, she slipped back and forth like a little mouse, discreetly clearing out the bulk of what she would need. But you all know the story; it's been told a thousand times and distorted ten times more. It was never Véra's intention to spawn a legend laced with endless miraculous events, far from it. If I'm here to tell you anything, it is this simple truth. The story of a young, bright, free woman in her thirties, who suddenly decided to follow her intuition. She saw, she sensed, she knew that the worst was yet to come. Her vision pounced on her with the same precision and ferocity of a lion tackling a gazelle. Humanity's future appeared before her as an irrepressible surge to the dark side. The feeling overwhelmed her completely, but she was unable to put it into words. Even if she could, who would she have told? She would have been written off as a nutjob. Realising it was better to preach in the wilderness than to wallow in the loony bin, she did what she knew was necessary. She stayed silent, at least until the moment she would have to pass on her crazy plan to the next man or woman in line. Véra was a believer. But she did not place her faith in God. She placed it in radio and in humanity; one and the same thing, as far as she was concerned.

This all happened in 2013. My father was aged one, and my grandfather, Véra's →

→ brother, was living at the family home in Longjumeau. She moved out of her tiny studio flat in Belleville and did up the property's disused outbuildings. In this hideaway she slowly started making her dream a reality, all the while working for 20 more years with RFI, first at Issy-les-Moulineaux, then further afield, each building more modern and less soulful than the last. Véra loved life. She smiled a lot. Despite being fully committed to her plan – or perhaps because of it – she was light-hearted and happy. That said, her life did become a lot more cloistered, and she never settled down with a partner or had children.

In 2035, the invention of the hypernet was the death knell for all other broadcast media. Less than five years later, there was no more FM and no more digital TV. It was impossible to broadcast anything without going through the Unified Global Network. The sinister UGN had just come under the control of the Great Global Conglomerate, itself established following the purchase (there's no other word for it) of the United Nations by a consortium made up of Google, Facebook, Amazon, Apple, the FSB, the 14K and Sun Yee On Triads, the Sinaloa Cartel, the Sicilian-Nigerian mafia and ISIS. Totalitarianism on an unprecedented scale. A world alliance of criminals, oligarchs and tech giants set against a backdrop of bankrupt nation states. But what's the point in making you relive these things you've lived through first-hand. Who among us – the survivors of the radio revolution – hasn't seen a video of a family member being decapitated, playing on loop over the hypernet? Who hasn't suffered in both body and soul at the hands of this ghastly digital regime?

With her customary stealth and dexterity, Véra managed to evade the surveillance apparatus of a system that arrogantly presumed to have co-opted every last remnant of reality in the world. In those days, there were still a few activists left – heirs of the Arab Spring, Wikileaks and Anonymous – who thought they could infiltrate the UGN. It took a while for them to realise that the internet, that great bastion of liberty, had become the most colossal prison in history, fronted by a bunch of criminals who seized power at the very moment the hypernet came into being. Véra alone understood, as she had for 20 years, that salvation would come from outside. She alone understood that, just as the internet had succeeded in toppling the old world order, so we would need to extricate ourselves from this web, to free ourselves from the monstrous, super-controlled society that it had brought about. Slipping under every radar, my great aunt managed, peacefully, to complete her task. All she had to do now was keep it alive, then hand it on.

I was born in 2045. In the blink of an eye, she knew, I was to be her Luke Skywalker, her Neo, her John Connor. The year she retired saw RFI fold, like all the other radio stations before it. Once and for all, the masters of the hypernet had eliminated every last media outlet that they had not created themselves. She spent the 50s picking through junk shops for old long-, medium- and short-wave transistor radios. As soon as I was old enough, I went along with her. Then, when I turned 13, she let me in on her secret and made me her successor. I was to continue the revolt. I cannot put into words the strange feeling that came over me the day she cranked open the iron shutter that kept her studio sealed from the world. The moment she switched on the lights, I realised my destiny. Four years later, when she died, I knew all there was to know about radio. It happened gradually, airing first to the area south of Paris before stretching further and further to the outer reaches of Europe and the Maghreb. I distributed radio sets, doggedly established a network and installed transmitters in the more remote regions. The rest was child's play. I just had to borrow some old insurrectionist techniques from the Paris banlieues of 2005 and the Arab Spring, then adopt the spirit of Radio Londres, the radio platform used by General de Gaulle in London a century before my birth to appeal to the French resistance with the rallying cry: "This is London Calling! The French speaking to the French!"

In 2065, on my twentieth birthday, I made my first broadcast. Sitting alone in the late Véra's studio, smiling like I had the first time I set foot in there, I uttered the words that would change everything: "This is Paris calling! The humans speaking to the humans!"

The rest you all know. The thugs of the GGC were only equipped to spy on the hypernet. No one had foreseen such a low-tech revolution, and they certainly hadn't expected it to

Once and for all, the masters of the hypernet had eliminated every last media outlet that they had not created themselves

bring down their psychopathic regime. Twenty years had gone by since the last broadcast and they no longer had the technology to locate radio transmitters. Before they knew it, they had lost ground across most of the globe. The war was awful. We lost a lot of people, but in the end we overthrew that wicked system. For this generation at least.

In recreating the studio where Véra worked in 2013, and in bringing you all here today, I am asking you never to forget where the uprising began. The spark was ignited here, before the enemy even existed. Never forget that it started under the red light of this deliciously vintage digital clock, under the mournful, slightly booze-addled eye of my great aunt, the woman who would become the architect of our newly won freedom.

*Translated by **Sam Gordon***

__Karim Miské__ is a documentary maker and novelist who lives in Paris. His latest novel translated into English is Arab Jazz. He tweets @karimmiske

The war of the words

46(01): 98/102 I DOI: 10.1177/0306422017703625

For the past few years **Amira Hanafi** has been gathering definitions of words for her project A Dictionary of the Revolution. The extracts from her dictionary, published here, reflect Egyptians' attitudes towards freedom of expression. **Sally Gimson** talks to Hanafi about the project

ABOVE: Amira Hanafi has been in Cairo since 2010, where she observed the Arab Spring and its aftermath

AMERICAN-EGYPTIAN WRITER AND artist Amira Hanafi has been working on an online project called A Dictionary of the Revolution, a memory archive of the Arab Spring in Egypt, often called "the uprising" locally, and its aftermath.

The project was born out of her desire to capture the voices of Egyptians between 2011 and 2013, when people started speaking out in public for the first time in many years.

Before the revolution people didn't talk much about their political views in public, said Hanafi. The years following the revolution were different. Public political speech was suddenly commonplace, so much so that the streets were filled with voices, expressing conflicting and shifting opinions on the developing events. It is these discussions, which were taking place in public places among ordinary people, that Hanafi was so keen to capture in her project. They're especially significant now when freedom of expression is still being threatened in Egypt by successive regimes, as seen by the arrest of 25 journalists between 1 January and 1 December 2016, according to the Committee to Protect Journalists.

In 2014, Hanafi and her team talked to around 200 people across several areas of Egypt (the Delta, Upper Egypt, Cairo, Alexandria and the Sinai peninsula) to try and get a representative sample of people's voices. She chose words like "freedom", "security", "revolution" and "couch party" (the latter referring to those who didn't participate in protests, but who went out into the →

Public political speech was suddenly commonplace, so much so that the streets were filled with voices, expressing conflicting and shifting opinions on the developing events

→ streets in 2013) and tried to find out how they defined these words.

"My concern is about those voices getting heard, not to highlight a particular opinion, but to let many opinions be heard. That is always on my mind," she told Index.

Although of Egyptian origin, Hanafi was brought up just outside New York. Egyptian-Arabic is her second language, which meant that when she moved to Cairo in 2010 she did not understand everything being said to her.

When she asked people about what words meant, they not only explained the word, but the history and social meaning behind the words. This prompted her to think about how she could capture the political debate through them.

Here we publish extracts from Hanafi's dictionary, which is due out in Arabic this Spring. These extracts have not yet been published in English. They are an amalgam of different people's views on each term, designed to be read as separate thoughts, yet sharing a common theme. ⊗

Sally Gimson is a freelance journalist

Definitions sourced for A Dictionary of the Revolution

Couch Party

WHEN THE REVOLUTION happened and nearly everyone took a position, the people who didn't were called the "couch party". They all sat on the couch and watched TV; they didn't do anything.

Their only objective was stability. These people wanted peace, nothing more and nothing less. It didn't matter to them if there was a certain president or a certain minister. For example, when Mubarak spoke on the night of 1 February 2011, saying he fully intended to leave power in six months' time, I imagine a large number of people said, "OK, just give him a chance."

I understand that some people are afraid of change. When the idea of revolution came up, it was really radical. Suddenly, there was intense change. People were talking about the removal of the regime. There were no police in the street. I feel as if fear was controlling people, to the point that they would accept any situation, no matter what happened.

Seventy million Egyptians are in the "couch party". And I want to say that they shouldn't be called the "couch party". They don't have another choice; their lives are forced upon them. They're always looking to put food on the table, and at the end of the day they go home to sleep without dinner, because they can't even accomplish that.

I was in the "couch party". I didn't participate in any democratic action, but not because I didn't want to. It was rather, why should I expend all this effort? What am I going to exhaust myself for? The whole process is completely fixed.

I was one of them at first, until I saw people dying in front of me on the television, so I did something.

We went out and participated, and we were happy about it, because we felt at the time, during those three years, that when we spoke our voices had value. In the end it became clear that the "couch party" had the loudest voice, and they defined Egypt's fate.

Freedom

OUR COUNTRY HAS a long way to go to achieve real freedom. But after the revolution, there's more than there was before.

We dreamed that freedom would be realised in Egypt.

For three years, I would give my opinion. I went out, participated and said, "I want this. Stop that. I don't want that."

There was more freedom of expression then, but these days it's being repressed.

There's no freedom of opinion, no freedom of expression, nothing at all. It's just survival of the fittest. The strong beats the weak.

I'm supposed to be able to speak up about anything that goes on in this country, because it's about me and my family, it's about my brother, my friends, it's about everyone. We still haven't got there. Not yet.

Now we've gone back to the beginning. If we take a look at what's happening now, whoever comes out and gives their opinion is stopped and is killed.

When was the best time you lived in your life? Wasn't it when Mubarak was in power? In my opinion, it was better. Yeah, he stole and pillaged from us, but we lived in safety. The police were working. If I were sitting here talking with you about something like this, at the time we would have been arrested. It wasn't right! But with people like us, that's the right thing.

All of my life, I've tried to live in a way that I'm free. But I have to be prepared to run into problems with people. People have had a problem accepting difference, before the revolution and after.

The things that used to be forbidden and that I do now without anyone judging me - that's freedom.

There's no room for freedom under the rule of a tyrant. It's like they can't rule the country while people feel their freedom. They have to be enslaved and feel that they're weak.

Freedom comes from inside the individual, not from outside. You have to believe in your freedom, and we're not convinced of ours. →

Voice

I IMAGINE WHAT'S meant by voice is your opinion. Your opinion spoken in a loud voice, one that's listened to, people pay attention to it.

The voice is always heard. I mean, so long as someone raises their voice, the country will stay alive, and no-one can silence the people, ever.

I don't know. Some time ago I felt that whatever we voiced, it was never heard.

The voice belongs to the demonstration. As long as there's a large number, the voice will get to where it's going. And no one can restrain that voice, as long as what they're saying is right.

The voices of the youth when they were in the square, chanting: "Raise, raise, raise your voice; whoever chants will not die."

"A woman's voice is not a sin." They used to say that a lot in the demonstrations.

After the revolution, the voice got to have a value. Before the revolution, even when we in civil society would raise an issue, organise a conference and meet with people, that would be the end of it. No one would bring up the subject again. But now when you say that something is an issue, you speak, you make groups on Facebook, you do other things, your voice is heard.

Now in the conditions we live in, there is no voice at all. This way or that, my voice has no value. Whoever speaks is trampled down. Now we find informants at the university with us, they find out who's who and what they're doing. If you think back to the Mubarak era, one had to sneak around and talk.

It's boredom and despair. That's what extinguishes the voice. Not gunfire or imprisonment. Boredom and despair.

Amira Hanafi is an artist and writer, and lives in Cairo. She is the author of Minced English (2010), Forgery (2011) and A Dictionary of the Revolution (2017)

THE UNICORN THEATRE IS PROUD TO SUPPORT THE FREEDOM OF EXPRESSION AWARDS 2017

Since 1947, the UK's leading theatre for young audiences has offered children the chance to experience exciting and innovative new theatre that is made just for them. The Unicorn's mission is to create great theatre that stimulates ideas and debate, and asks us to consider how we might better live with ourselves and with one another.

UNICORN

147 TOOLEY STREET, LONDON SE1 2HZ ⊖ ⇄ LONDON BRIDGE
020 7645 0560 · UNICORNTHEATRE.COM

Supported using public funding by
ARTS COUNCIL
ENGLAND

Crimean closedown

46(01): 104/109 | DOI: 10.1177/0306422017703626

Crimean writer **Vyacheslav Huk** can't find a publisher for his work in his native land because it is written in Ukrainian. Translator **Stephen Komarnyckyj** introduces an extract from his latest reworked novel, The Garden of Galatea, and a poem from his Crimean Elegies collection

NOVELIST AND POET Vyacheslav Huk was born in 1974 in Saki, a mainly Russian-speaking town in Crimea. But his commitment to writing in Ukrainian and his fascination with other European literature have set him at odds with the pro-Russian government controlling his birthplace. His work is now unpublishable in his native land.

The new government in Crimea has removed Ukrainian from schools. Ukrainian media is banned because it "doesn't correspond to Russian legislation" and Reuters reports that the only Ukranian language library in Russia is closing.

The Crimean publishing industry has understood that the seizure of the peninsula by the Russians has rendered the publication and marketing of Ukrainian books unfeasible. Bookshops have ceased stocking publications in the language and demand has plummeted.

Even though Ukrainian is officially a state language, Crimea's Ukrainian speaking population have almost no access to books in their own tongue. The language is being strangled.

For Huk, this is a particular tragedy. In 2008, the first version of his novel Sad Halatyi (The Garden of Galatea) was published in Crimea. When a massively revised version of the same novel emerged in 2015, it was only published in the Ukrainian capital Kiev.

Fellow poet Dmytro Pavlychko has compared Huk's writing to the German writer Thomas Mann and the Argentine short story writer and essayist Jorge Luis Borges. Huk's novel The Garden of Galatea is an elegy for obsessive love similar to that portrayed in Mann's Death in Venice and a first person account of dehumanisation, which has echoes of Borges' Deutsches Requiem.

Like most of Huk's work, the novel, while written in Ukrainian, is not about Ukraine. Its protagonist, Asar Janson, is one of the tiny number of Jews who clandestinely joined the SS, and it is set mainly in Latvia.

Asar sets fire to an old people's home on 4 November 2006 possibly killing Marta, with whom he was obsessively in love. He tells the story of his life in a self-serving manner, sprinkling it with historical and literary allusions. We are never sure how accurate his recollections are, nor of the degree of his participation in the Holocaust. The novel is a subtle portrayal of how complicity in evil corrodes memory and the possibility of love.

In the passage translated below we hear Asar Janson narrating a memory of a memory. During his post-war life with Marta, he dreams frequently about the Holocaust. He remembers how he used alcohol and misogynistic sex in an attempt to blank out the horrors he saw. He is grieving over the loss

OPPOSITE: Men believed to be Russian soldiers guard a Ukrainian military base in Simferopol, Crimea, shortly after the annexation in 2014

Crimea's Ukrainian-speaking population have almost no access to books in their own tongue. The language is being strangled

of his humanity. His voice is a metaphor for Ukraine and eastern Europe's troubled past.

As well as an extract from The Garden of Galatea, Index is publishing exclusively in English a poem from Huk's Krymski Elehii (Crimean Elegies), a poetry collection that came out in 2013. The poetry contains little about Crimea, but focuses presciently on war and exile. It now reads as if Huk anticipated his sadness and feelings of bereavement at the severance of his birthplace from Ukraine.

The reference in the poem Birds to a "military Grasshopper", a World War II-era plane, feels like an augury of war. The poem also alludes to Greek mythology, part of Crimea's heritage and its perhaps lost European future. ⊗

Steve Komarnyckyj is a translator, writer and poet →

Extract from The Garden of Galatea

MARTA LEFT THE verandah and I remained seated at the table, although I was very tired. I reflected on how our unclean thoughts writhed through our brains. They were like obese worms, concealed by the fine linen of our skin as clothing masks our venial bodies. Our life consists of acts that are and always were mundane and simultaneously insane. The dependency on something or other that had the same value as manure. I was filled with a demented yearning for someone who could understand and listen to my spirit, but who? Marta? No, unfortunately this woman was only interested in the possibility of having a family with me. It was as if she were a flower, or a female tree, which needed to continue its species. I had no wish to be the equivalent of pollen…

I have a free spirit. At that moment I wanted to become a chrysalis, to disappear from Marta's view… yes, it was imperative to flee as fast as possible, to be anywhere but here…

Delighted at this pleasant thought I hummed a now almost forgotten song and went to bed.

I open the window wide and I shed my clothes, although the nights near the estuary had become cold in anticipation of autumn. I lie on the creaking bed and close my eyes, crossing my hands on my breast like a corpse silvered by moonlight, and pondered. It would be good if this house had not only windows but a glass ceiling. Then all the stars in the sky, and not just that portion looming tranquilly at the window, would be visible. With my closed eyes I had a vivid glimpse of the muddy, unwelcoming waters of the estuary in the morning. They quietly bore driftwood onto the sands, the rubbish that the sea proffers for the thoughts of those who will view it later. They will ponder what structure those fragments were once part of. Only time transforms a happy song into a funeral dirge and renders molasses saline and toxic.

I open my eyes and see the black, motionless gauze of night studded with minute, copper-tinged stars. The bird concealed under my ribs had long become calm. She no longer strove for an unnecessary and extremely dangerous freedom. I would write a note for Marta and flee, thereby saving myself from this overwhelming melancholy and utter solitude forever. Marta unbalanced me, like a mechanism with her sharp, painful words and unconsidered acts. However, she would never seize my treasured liberty.

I struggled to get to sleep, but dreams mingled with reality, resembling a kind of delirium, though I am aware that this is, in fact, an old memory. I see the train station in some town and glittering railway lines that fly towards the West. I am wearing a German military uniform. For some reason there are no wagons at the station. The railway workers, who have been shot, have been laid near the buffet. Insects, viscous and black, buzzed and swarmed over the swollen and mutilated corpses. Nausea gripped me. It was stiflingly hot outside, like a blazing July day. I felt the need to use the toilets and found them quickly. All the rancid holes for human waste were occupied. Footsteps. I heard the train throbbing. I listened to the slithering sound of the water in the broken sink. They dragged people into these holes while they were still alive and tortured them for a protracted period. Then finally they murdered them. Paper signs were tied to their legs and inscribed with the words "Jude, Jüdin, Verräter, Prostituierte..." I pulled someone's headless body by its legs from one of the holes. My eyes fixed on the white vertebra and the black blood, still warm, upon it. I had no spittle with which to wet my burning lips. I dragged more and still more men, women and children onto the tiled floor that was wet with blood and vomit. One dark-complexioned teenager still had the inscription "Jude, Jüdin, Verräter, Prostituierte..." attached to her. Her head was partially severed but still somehow attached to her neck muscles. I wept quietly. My tears were as sticky as the blood soiling my hands.

Marta unbalanced me, like a mechanism with her sharp, painful words and unconsidered acts

I went out into the street where tall poplar trees reached into the sky. The faint sun slept in the dark birds' nests among their tangled branches. It was difficult. Terrifying. Repellent. There was fresh blood on my soldier's boots. As if I were a slaughterhouse operative who had just emerged from the abattoir having deprived a cow, pig or sheep of its life. My heart was torn to pieces by darkness and anguish. I stopped, pulled off my boots, threw them into a hawthorn bush and roamed in my bare feet, aimless and stupefied. That same night I downed a few tumblers of strong, pungent vodka to forget everything around me. I fucked dementedly with some slut from the East I had bought for a bottle of something, as if this transgression would be the last act of my life. Later I remembered with fear and shame how I had adopted postures in bed that would have been worthy of a gifted acrobat. Yes, it was simply repulsive.

And the next day everything was repeated. I had agreed to meet with this whore at roughly four o'clock in the afternoon by a dilapidated hangar. The structure had once been used for military vehicles and smelled of fuel and sodden timber. However, the lady was late or, more accurately, we were both late. In that dark hangar, designated for very old vehicles, I tried somehow to quieten my sullied desire to make love. I stood on the hood of a Willys Jeep looking who knows where and then pressed my body into the body of the whore I had →

→ bought. Ants ran down my spine as we touched. I enfolded the whore in my appalling embrace. As if in some tainted, ambiguous dream I inhaled the gentle fragrance of her hair and skin. I unfolded her from her dress and pulled off her underwear. The hooker tensed as if she was a respectable woman, but this was for show. There, on the hood, in a drunken lust I took her. Grabbing her arm, kissing her frantically, spreading her legs. It seemed then that I was too simple, too ordinary to do what I did.

I made myself repulsive to myself for a moment. I remembered how, to begin with, I drank an aperitif accompanied by slices of lemon with her for quite a while in some cafe. Then the clock on the old town hall rang for half past six and sounds muted by evening melted into the autumn sky. We went, already pretty drunk, to the hangar. We misused it as if it were a room reserved in a hotel. However, everything was a little better than the year before when I tried to make love in the overnight compartment of a fast train to Riga. That night then finally defined the genuine, strange scope of my love and diseased longing for voluptuous women.

The floor beneath our feet was fetid, dank and dirty. It was far from an attractive place for such an occupation. However, I rapidly took control of this woman, ridding myself forever of the impression that these couplings, purchased for a glass of wine, were mechanical in nature. I became predatory to forget that I was a human being. My body sweated intensely and profusely. The whore moaned, surrendering herself to the brutal force of just another ordinary man. I tried to stimulate her and my sensations so we could break free of life's ugly truth momentarily... and forget all in the weird morphine of bogus love. Her kisses prickled my lips. Her tears were sticky on my cheeks. I was in some warm, tranquil bay on an ordinary boat. The tangled hair of this woman was a breeze for my sail, its touch hot on my skin. At each thrust I tried to reach the essence of a life that I had lost somewhere, but distanced myself from the truth still more. I worked at that lady as if she were a complex, but very desirable, job.

Every time I had intercourse with these bought women it seemed to me that I lost part of myself. I gave myself to them, to satisfy my body's needs. When a very drunk, lusty whore satisfied with this lovemaking weeps quietly, her arms clasping her arms around my neck, I whispered utter nonsense... that this scene should be portrayed with the eyes of an artist. That it is necessary to look into yourself when you feel oppressed. To be with that person you love so strongly, in spite of separation, war and borders. The biological right of men and women to be with one another monogamously is unrealisable for us now. How, I asked my lovers, can you obey that biological instinct when some force pulls you backwards and forwards? A force that never ceases, for there is a certain boundary beyond which all that is most important loses significance. Where body and soul alike are subject to the extreme physical aggression that occurs during war.

Then a typical woman becomes bio material. A piston simply enters its allocated socket. That's how procreation occurs at such times and you lose yourself utterly as a human being.

Birds

This late summer, and the melody of song protracted,
Like soothing words or victory after struggle,
A planned assault or the delusions of Penelope,
Wherein distant perspectives are awash with birds,
And a military Grasshopper
Disappears into the sky and fades to unconsciousness,
A coffee's warm vapour drifts from one of the tables,
And a white rose exhales its fragrance.
You are entitled to all of this,
The wind subdued by the tree's dark tree crown
Forms melodies of yellow leaves,
Extracted from a box, whether for an undefined period,
A short August vacation abroad.
The engine hums through broken passages of summer,
Where the wind cradles birds' nests in tree crowns,
Giving you the possibility to whisper: this is an augury
Or the comprehension of an image and the end point of flight
Which remains dark and immutable in any season.
The negative of a plane bombing a foreign location.
Through all horizons, without exception, and in all perspectives,
The low sky you encompass in a glance continues
With a plane at a high altitude, and there is no possibility
Of analysing life's boundlessness in dreams.
So you watch birds through binoculars,
Their wings sculling through blue sky,
Anticipating autumn's coldness
As they fly towards the southern coast.

*Translated by **Steve Komarnyckyj***

Vyacheslav Huk *is an award-winning writer from the Crimea, Ukraine. He is the author of several books of poetry and fiction*

Index around the world

INDEX NEWS

46(01): 110/113 | DOI: 10.1177/0306422017703628

Kieran Etoria-King introduces new projects covering free speech on campus and censorship in the arts, as well as the latest details about the Index awards and the nominees

THERE ARE TWO things the Index awards focus on; the courage and creativity of people doing things against the odds, such as Behrouz Boochani, a refugee and journalist from Iran, who continues to work from Australia's Manus Island detention centre. So said Index on Censorship's head of fellowship David Heinemann, describing the nominations for the upcoming Index awards.

"In every single one of these cases, they're all David and Goliath stories," said Heinemann.

For the past few months judges including actor Noma Dumezweni, lawyer Caoilfhionn Gallagher, magazine editor Tina Brown, technologist Anab Jain and co-founder of Africa Express Stephen Budd, along with Index staff, have been examining this year's 387 nominations. The shortlist was published on 7 February and the winners will be announced on 19 April at a gala at the Unicorn Theatre, London.

When researching the stories of the hundreds of nominees, Heinemann noticed some trends, one being a clear move towards government internet shutdowns, and even potentially power cuts and shortages in different parts of the world, which are used as a tool to clamp down on free speech. "There is beginning to be a fightback against that as people clock what's happening," he said.

"Another trend is the ongoing plight of refugees, who are often struggling not only for a home and for a profession, but for their very identities and to be seen as people in their own right with valued professions and skills of their own."

In other news, Index on Censorship magazine welcomed its new deputy editor Jemimah Steinfeld in January. Steinfeld, who has been writing for the magazine since 2013 and was also a contributing editor, previously lived and worked in China.

Asked what she thinks her time living in Beijing and Shanghai will bring to Index, she said: "I worked for media that is based in China and so is directly censored, as well as writing for international media where you can speak and write more freely but you always worry about your visa, so I bring a very direct experience of what it means to be censored."

She added: "Having seen the effects of what censorship can do to a society, how it can affect so much, from people's relationships to the education structure, you realise that this isn't a trivial matter, this isn't something to be taken for granted." →

OPPOSITE: Yemeni street artist Murad Subay accepts his Freedom of Expression Award in 2016

CREDIT: Elina Kansikast

CREDIT: Above: Sean Gallagher Right: Nigel Smith/Council of Europe

→ Julia Farrington, associate arts producer at Index on Censorship, will lead a new project that looks at art and offence. In partnership with arts network What Next? and the social enterprise Cause4, it will provide training to tackle self-censorship for board members and directors of galleries,

This isn't a trivial matter, this isn't something to be taken for granted

theatres, museums and other artistic spaces.

"Our hope is really that we will encourage people to take more risks," Farrington said. "We have to accept, and I think most people would, that we live in a risk averse culture, that we have let risk aversion be seen as a virtue. I think many people would say that it's gone too far, that we are over protective in lots of areas."

The project will work with leaders in the

arts to help update them on laws that might affect their ability to produce a show or exhibition.

Farrington said: "When you have a controversial idea, and you don't want it to just spin out of control into public protest, press furore and that sort of thing, what do you need to do to put that controversial idea into enough context, and get enough voices who are affected by the idea, and give value to the different sides of the argument that may be offended or hostile?"

Another new strand of Index work is the Free Speech on Campus research project. Senior advocacy officer Melody Patry launched this project as free speech at universities is particularly under threat at present. Articles in this issue by Jan Fox on US universities (page 29) and Natasha Joseph on South Africa (page 18) highlight this.

"Recently there has been an increase in incidents of restrictions on speech in universities worldwide," Patry explained. "Our research project will focus on the UK and USA, and will examine these restrictions and the impact they have."

As part of a separate project, in April Patry and Hannah Machlin, project officer for Mapping Media Freedom, which charts attacks on journalists in 42 countries, will travel to Ukraine to attend a meeting of the Council of Europe's Platform for the Protection of Journalism and the Safety of Journalists.

"Every quarter we meet to discuss cases that have been filed, opportunities to re-invest and to identify positive outcomes," said Patry.

"This time we will meet in Kiev. In the past Ukraine was one of the deadliest countries for reporters. Things have got better, but there are still some problems in places like Crimea. The Council of Europe have taken the matter in hand and want to take the opportunity to make improvements."

While this platform is focused on Europe, Patry also attended MisinfoCon, a summit held by the Nieman Foundation for Journalism at Harvard and MIT Media Lab in February. The summit looked at trust, verification and fact-checking, with a goal to connect leaders and develop steps to held

improve trust and tackle misinformation.

Finally the winter issue of the magazine, featuring the Fashion Rules special report, was launched in an event hosted by Google at their headquarters in London. One of Index's largest ever audiences for a magazine

Our hope is really that we will encourage people to take more risks

launch came along to debate with a panel including magazine contributors Maggie Alderson and Laura Silvia Battaglia, plus fashion historian Amber Butchart and New African Woman editor Regina Jane Jere-Malanda. They discussed topics including the misogyny of corporate and religious dress codes, resistance to uniformity, and the recent trend away from rebellion in Western fashion. ⊗

Kieran Etoria-King is the current Liverpool John Moores/Tim Hetherington fellow. He is the editorial assistant at Index on Censorship

OPPOSITE: Murad Subay and Index CEO Jodie Ginsberg painting a mural in London, April 2016

LEFT: Melody Patry with Council of Europe commissioner for human rights Niels Muiznieks during the Losing Our Rights event in Strasbourg, January 2017

Getting print out

END NOTE

46(01): 114/116 | DOI: 10.1177/0306422017703629

Crowdsourcing is helping authors get their books directly to audiences when traditional publishers are worried about government pressure, writes **Jemimah Steinfeld**

IT LOOKED LIKE Mei Fong had hit a dead-end with publishing her book in China. The Pulitzer Prize-winning journalist was generating a lot of buzz for the English language-version of One Child: The Story of China's Most Radical Experiment. But in China, where there would be a massive readership for her book, she struggled to get a publisher.

"I approached a couple of people who had books published in Taiwan, and [the publishers] came back saying: 'Sorry, it's an important book, but we have to consider market forces'."

By market forces, they were hinting that the Chinese government was likely to block the book's publication in China. Fong encountered a similar story elsewhere, and it was once she had exhausted all of her options that she turned to self-publishing. While not new, the opportunities that the digital age brings, including crowdfunding, are changing the rules of self-publishing. These rules are opening spaces up, especially for those wanting to publish in highly censored environments.

For Fong, self-publishing was not something she considered when the book was first commissioned in 2012. The publishing arm of major Chinese company Citic wanted to acquire the China publishing rights, so long as they could put the book through the normal Chinese censorship machine. But Fong didn't accept. She wanted to keep her options open and assumed there would be other offers at a later date.

But by the end of 2012, there was a presidential transition period from Hu Jintao to Xi Jinping under way. When the book came out in English three years later, the situation had drastically changed. Xi has overseen a tightening of censorship within China. Even in Hong Kong, a more typical publishing route for those with books that might rattle Chinese censors, the situation was not healthy. By this stage, the forced disappearance of five Hong Kong booksellers had been reported.

"I thought it would come to the point where someone would publish it, but would want it to be censored. I wasn't even given that choice," Fong said.

The two biggest barriers for Fong were translation and distribution. Translation was not only very expensive, but it also raised the issue of who would translate the book willingly. Finally, a translator agreed to do it on condition of anonymity.

As for distribution, Fong did not have a Chinese bank account. Even if she did, she was wary of monetary transactions, as one of the arrested Hong Kong booksellers had been released only on the condition that he revealed who had bought books at his store. Fong did not want to create a similar paper trail.

She finally decided to release the book as

a free PDF, which she uploaded to Weixin, an instant-messaging service and blog, and other platforms. The main ambition was to get it read widely, though Fong has little way of gauging this marker of success. She knew she would lose control in this respect, which was partly the point – for it to be distributed without a trace. She has received some positive feedback from Chinese people who have read it, though.

She also crowdfunded to cover some of her costs, such as for the translation, which was approximately $10,000. So far, she has covered one third.

"One of the things I am saying is we need more well-funded avenues for this," said Fong, adding that while it was not a

I thought it would come to the point where someone would publish it, but would want it to be censored. I wasn't even given that choice

money-making endeavour, she wanted to show that you could earn money through writing of this nature, as it might encourage others.

Fong's example isn't the only one of on-line publication solving two author issues – censorship and costs. In Iran, for example, the publishing house Nogaam is behind many titles by authors who know they have little chance of being published there →

ABOVE: A man reads at a bookstore in Beijing, China, where censorship of literature is commonplace

→ otherwise due to censorship. Its business model also involves crowdfunding. Once an author has been compensated, the book is available free via download.

"If you're in Iran and your book is rejected or censored to the bone then you had to either bin it or put it on a shelf to gather dust. So online publishers like Nogaam are giving people a new choice," Nogaam editor Azadeh Iravani told The Guardian.

Mark Coker is the founder of Smashwords, which is one of the largest distributors of independent ebooks. Smashwords distributes the majority of its books to major ebook retailers and libraries in the USA. It also operates its own small online store. Coker's company arose when he was unable to sell his book to publishers because they did not see its market potential.

What would happen to culture if readers were allowed to read only what was most popular?

"The experience opened my eyes to what I viewed as a horrible problem that represented a threat to books and book culture. What would happen to culture if readers were allowed to read only what was most popular? Such a focus leads to loss of diversity of thought, knowledge and opinion," Coker told Index.

Coker explains how even in Western countries, there has been a crackdown on publishing erotic literature, such as books that deal with incest, bestiality or rape. As fiction, these books are legal in many countries, yet they're not socially acceptable. In 2012, for example, Smashwords was told by PayPal to delete fiction that concerned these topics, or be refused service. Upon negotiation with Smashwords, PayPal changed its terms of policy to allow this type of fiction. It was hailed as a victory for free speech,

as it removed payment processors from the business of book censorship.

Some retailers still refuse to carry these books for fear of offending their customers or damaging their public reputations. To remedy this situation, Smashwords allows these authors to sell books in the small online Smashwords store. Smashwords wanted to protect the ability of all authors to publish, said Coker, and to offer ways for them to be financed.

"Although I may personally find these more taboo subjects revolting, I consider myself a defender of free speech and a defender of a reader's right to experience fantasies in the safety of their own mind. If it's acceptable for a reader to read a thriller and experience the mindset of a serial murderer or terrorist, then why can't they experience sexual fantasies in the privacy of their own mind?" said Coker.

But even if epublishing does offer more options for authors, it is still hard to cover costs, let alone make any money. Crowdsourcing and the marketing that goes with it takes a lot of time, and targets are often just to cover the running costs. What's more, it is still not an option for everyone. Fong admitted that there's a strong chance she wouldn't be granted a visa for China in the future; it's a loss she factored into the project.

Meanwhile in Bangladesh, where the market for online publishing has seen several writers launch themselves, Sadaf Saaz, a director of Dhaka Lit Fest, said writers self-published at their own risk.

"It could be that if publishers were to refuse then self-publishing would be an option, but writers themselves are being threatened, too, so publishing on issues such as atheism has its risks, whether officially published by a publishing house or on one's own," Saaz told Index. ⊗

Jemimah Steinfeld is deputy editor of Index on Censorship magazine